D1497936

DATE DUE

~~NOV 07 1994~~			
~~NOV 28 1994~~			
GAYLORD			PRINTED IN U.S.A.

The Texas Legacy of Katherine Anne Porter

The Texas Legacy of Katherine Anne Porter

by James T.F. Tanner

TEXAS WRITERS SERIES

NUMBER THREE

UNIVERSITY OF NORTH TEXAS PRESS

TEXAS WRITERS SERIES NUMBER THREE

General Editor James Ward Lee

Copyright © 1990 by James T. F. Tanner
All rights reserved
Printed in the United States of America
First Edition, 1991

Requests for permission to reproduce material from this work should be sent to the University of North Texas Press, P.O. Box 13856, Denton, Texas 76203–3856.

The paper in this book meets the minimum requirements of the American National Standard for Permanence of Paper for Printed Library Materials, Z39.48–1984.

Library of Congress Cataloging-in-Publication Data

Tanner, James T. F., 1937-
    The Texas Legacy of Katherine Anne Porter / by James T.F. Tanner.—1st ed.
        p. cm. — (Texas writers series : no. 3)
    Includes bibliographical references and index.
    ISBN 0–929398–22–X : $19.95
    1. Porter, Katherine Anne, 1890–1980—Criticism and interpretation. 2. Porter, Katherine Anne, 1890–1980—Knowledge—Texas. 3. Authors, American—20th century—Biography. 4. Texas in literature. 5. Texas—Biography. I. Title. II. Series.
PS3531.0752Z825 1990
813'.52—dc20
                                            90–23052
                                                CIP

FOR JANE LEE HINKLE TANNER

TABLE OF CONTENTS

FOREWORD

During the composition of this critical study of Katherine Anne Porter, I have kept in mind the projected major emphasis of the books to appear in the Texas Writers Series—the influence of the Texas place on the author, focusing on writers whose Texas connections have not been fully examined. There is, of course, no lack of secondary scholarship and criticism on the life and work of Katherine Anne Porter; but scholarly and critical study of the relationship between Porter's fiction and her Texas background has not by any means been exhausted. Katherine Anne Porter fits precisely, therefore, into the emphasis of the Texas Writers Series; it is exactly that—the Texas connection—that has not yet been extensively treated. I am particularly concerned with Porter's seeming *denial* of her Texas heritage, her apparent urge to distance herself from Texas and all things Texan—an urge that apparently led her to re-create herself into the being she would like to have been, while disavowing her real identity. This self-made myth of Katherine Anne Porter is fascinating in itself, and of considerable importance for students of Texas culture. For this reason, I have focused continuously on Porter's settings and characters, attempting to emphasize and clarify the influence of the Texas upbringing on her creative art. Still, I understand the risk of provincialism involved in a study of this sort. The reader will note that I title the book *The Texas Legacy of Katherine Anne Porter*; the central tension in Porter's work is, it seems to me, the conflict between the Texas Porter and the urbane-sophisticate Porter, the continual reference to her roots alongside the sometimes conscious, sometimes unconscious rejection of those roots. Her wanderings over the earth notwithstanding, Katherine Anne Porter was a Texas writer first and last.

In April of 1988, a three-day conference, titled "Katherine Anne Porter and Texas: An Uneasy Relationship," was hosted by Texas A&M University. Speaking at the conference were such notables as Cleanth Brooks, the distinguished "New Critic" and personal friend of Katherine Anne Porter; Joan Givner, author of *Katherine Anne Porter: A Life*, the definitive biography; Don Graham, a leading authority on Texas literature; Paul Porter, nephew of Katherine Anne Porter, who, as he candidly pointed out in quoting Gertrude Stein's remark of him, "has traveled far on his nephewship"; and Professors Darlene H. Unrue, Thomas Walsh, W. Craig Turner, and Mark Busby, all with interesting and important things to say about Katherine Anne Porter. Frank Vandiver, then President of Texas A&M, formally convened the conference by making a few offhand remarks about the unfortunate relationship between Katherine Anne Porter and the Texas Institute of Letters. The collection of essays based on this conference, *Katherine Anne Porter and Texas: An Uneasy Relationship*, edited by Clinton Machann and William Bedford Clark (Texas A&M University Press, 1990) is quite useful to anyone interested in the general subject of Katherine Anne Porter's relationship to Texas literature; especially helpful is Sally Dee Wade's select, annotated bibliography that lists primary and secondary sources documenting Porter's "Texas connection."

And yet the conference, despite the splendid gathering of critics well qualified in Porter scholarship, failed—it seems to me—to speak authoritatively on the "uneasy relationship" between Porter and Texas, the announced theme of the gathering.

This book, then, attempts to place Katherine Anne Porter as a Texas writer. Her national, perhaps even international reputation is already secure (no other Texas author has yet made it into the *Norton Anthology of World Masterpieces*). It is high time that the eyes of Texas should be upon her. When Porter was once told of Thomas Wolfe's insis-

tence that "you can't go home again," she responded
curtly, "Nonsense, it's the only place you can go."
Born in Indian Creek, Texas, in 1890, Katherine
Anne Porter was always a "Texas writer," even
though she roamed widely, and though she seemed
to represent, for many readers, a more "Southern"
and "genteel" facet of Texas culture than they were
prepared to accept. The "Southern" and "genteel"
features of her fiction have, in my opinion, been
overemphasized.

The format of this book will, I hope, facilitate the
work of students of Texas literature in general as
well as that of students interested in Katherine
Anne Porter's fiction. I have attempted to deal with
Katherine Anne Porter as a Texas storyteller.
Chapter 1 ("Katherine Anne Porter and Texas Let-
ters") is a discussion of the scholarly and critical
reception of Porter's work among the Texas literati.
Chapter 2 ("'A Little Girl from Texas': The Life of
Katherine Anne Porter") is a brief summary of the
Porter biography. Porter's fiction is discussed in
Chapter 3 ("Stories of Texas, the South, and South-
west") , Chapter 4 ("Stories of Mexico") , Chapter 5
("Stories of New York and New England") , Chapter
6 ("Stories of Germany: 'The Leaning Tower' and
Ship of Fools") . Chapter 7 ("Conclusion") is a brief
summation. The selected bibliography should help
readers to locate, easily and quickly, additional

sources of specific information. Space limitations
precluded a separate chapter on Porter's nonfiction,
but I have alluded—where relevant—to her essays,
reviews, translations, and speeches. I hope the book
can be used as a small manual on Katherine Anne
Porter as a Texas writer.

By way of acknowledgment, I must say that I, like
all modern students of Katherine Anne Porter, owe
an immense and unpayable debt to Joan Givner,
whose monumental *Katherine Anne Porter: A Life*
(1982) has recently corrected and revitalized Porter
studies. All Porter scholarship having anything
to do with biographical interpretation must now
be labeled either BG (before Givner) or AG (after
Givner). Among the numerous scholarly and critical
works on Katherine Anne Porter that I have found
useful, Willene and George Hendrick's *Katherine
Anne Porter: Revised Edition* (1988) is noteworthy.
And Ms. Blanche T. Ebeling-Koning, Curator of the
Katherine Anne Porter Collection at the University
of Maryland Library, has been most helpful, responding immediately to any and all requests for
assistance.

On a more personal note, I should like to thank
Professor James W. Lee, the General Editor of the
Texas Writers Series (as well as my department
chairman and personal friend) for his kindly encouragement and assistance. The Executive Committee

of the Department of English, and Alice Mathews, Assistant Chair of the English Department at the University of North Texas, have been kind in their accommodation of my requests for released time from teaching duties and for convenient course schedules. Fran Vick, Director of the University of North Texas Press, has been quite patient and understanding during the delays and dark nights of the soul that accompany any project of this kind. Most of all, I gratefully acknowledge the indispensable help of my wife Jane, a most excellent editor, proofreader, computer whiz, and counsellor; to her the book is dedicated.

1

KATHERINE ANNE PORTER AND
TEXAS LETTERS

Katherine Anne Porter's place in Texas letters is a matter of some contention.

In 1981, A. C. Greene, the influential Texas journalist, novelist, and critic, published in *Texas Monthly* an annotated list of "The Fifty Best Texas Books." Included in his list is Katherine Anne Porter's *Pale Horse, Pale Rider*. About this book Greene says,

> Some people say *Pale Horse, Pale Rider* (1939) is not a Texas book, but they forget, perhaps, that the volume of that title contains two other famous short novels, *Old Mortality* and *Noon Wine*, both with Texas settings. In any case, I don't care. I insist that *Pale Horse, Pale Rider* is the best Texas fiction ever written.

Greene went on to say that he had once met Katherine Anne Porter and was astonished to hear her deny that she had ever been a newspaper reporter anywhere in Texas. "I have always thought it strange," says Greene, "[that] she was so bitter in her disavowal of things Texan but did so many of her best stories with a Texas background" (6). Greene is certainly not alone in this regard.

Larry McMurtry, the only other Texas writer to attain national recognition, has had, throughout his career, to deal with the irritating presence of Katherine Anne Porter, frequently cited as "the only really great" writer ever to come out of Texas. It is not to be wondered at, then, that McMurtry—in those moments when he considers himself a "Texas writer"—yields to the temptation to exile her from his attention, and from consideration as a Texas writer at all. His barb in "Southwestern Literature?" is instructive: "Katherine Anne Porter was born in Indian Creek—can we then take credit for her better stories? I think not. Let those who are free of Texas enjoy their freedom" (*In a Narrow Grave* 31). But surely Texas is big enough for two "great" writers; and, whatever McMurtry may really think, Katherine Anne Porter was never—any more than McMurtry himself—really "free of Texas." Attempting to damn Porter with faint praise, McMurtry complained—in his controversial 1981 essay, "Ever a Bridegroom: Reflections on the Failure of Texas Literature,"—that "she was genteel to the core":

Oh, the whole talent was there, and a fine talent it was: but a talent seldom either fully or generously put to use. Miss Porter believed in a pure style; hers, at times, is purified almost to the vanishing point. By her account, she did this in the name of an aesthetic, removing the local and the immediate in order to reach the timeless and universal.

Unfortunately for her aesthetic, and unfortunately too for many of her stories, the local and immediate is the true street of fiction—at least of the sort of realistic fiction she was trying to write. (16)

Again, it appears that Porter's alleged disavowal of "the local and immediate" is of central concern to McMurtry as was her "disavowal of things Texan" to A. C. Greene.

The fact that Katherine Anne Porter has supplied most of McMurtry's competition for the title of "great writer of Texas" may even account for his attempt to direct the critics to Porter's nonfiction instead of her fiction. As he says, Katherine Anne Porter's

passionate, often vengeful essays now seem more alive and probably more permanent than all but a few of her stories. In attack she was

>   always quite confident, and far less genteel
>   (17).

No one will be taken in, of course. Porter's critical
stance was completely impressionistic, opinionated,
and sometimes genuinely wrongheaded; her reputation will stand or fall on her short fiction, not her
essays.

But Joan Givner has identified, probably correctly, another motive for McMurtry's rejection of
Katherine Anne Porter. Givner notes that Mc-
Murtry's description of Porter's "style" uses adjec-
tives with a decidedly antifeminist bias. McMurtry
accuses Porter of "boiling the accents of her own
time and place" out of her fiction (a kitchen metaphor); further, McMurtry describes the Porter style
as "powdery," and "elegant"—feminine images
again! He describes her as "genteel to the core"; but
he does curtsy in her direction by agreeing that occasionally "the artist won the battle with the lady."
Givner's devastating comments on this sort of criticism seem well advised. But even more interesting
is her connection of such commentary with J. Frank
Dobie's attitudes toward "Southwestern" literature,
and with Dobie's victory in 1939 over Porter in the
Texas Institute of Letters affair. "I would suggest,"
she says, "that the 'indigenous nature' of Dobie's
subject matter was that its masculinity conformed

more to the spirit of the West. There was none of that tremulous sensibility, that preoccupation with the inner world of the imagination, with relationships between men and women or with what George Eliot has called 'the roar the other side of silence'" (59–60). Porter's fiction was apparently not masculine enough for the Texas Institute of Letters.

Tom Pilkington, an academic authority on Texas literature, maintains that Katherine Anne Porter is the only "great" writer produced by the state:

> . . . let it be admitted, right off, that there have been no literary geniuses to emerge from Texas. . . . A possible exception to this generalization is Katherine Anne Porter—if . . . a case can be made for Porter's being branded a Texas writer, since she spent most of her literary life in voluntary and sometimes embittered exile from Texas. But maybe Porter is an exception, or a partial one—a potential genius, anyway, who wrote a handful of stunningly good stories, many of them set in Texas, that will be read as long as the English language and the printed word endure. Otherwise, I doubt that even the most optimistic Texas chauvinist would claim that the state has produced any truly great writers." (167–68)

It may be that Pilkington himself reveals an optimistic Texas chauvinism in this passage. But, again, the problem central to his concern is Porter's removal from the Texas world, not—as one might hope it would be—the text of her work. It is as if James Joyce could not be branded an Irish writer because of his prolonged absence from Ireland.

James Ward Lee's influential guide, *Classics of Texas Fiction* (1987), reviews forty-seven novels by thirty-eight of what Lee considers to be the finest Texas writers; he does not include Katherine Anne Porter. Lee notes in his preface that he deals only with novels, not with short fiction. Lee must be partially forgiven, since few would consider *Ship of Fools*, Porter's only full-length novel, worthy of inclusion. Lee notes, furthermore, that despite his admiration of Katherine Anne Porter's work, he does not think that she is "the only star in the Texas firmament" (xii-xiii). And, in justice to Lee's comment, one can see the harm that can be and has been done to Texas literary studies by constantly referring to Katherine Anne Porter's work as unsurpassable and classic. Surely, there must be many points of light in Texas letters. Nevertheless, it is to be lamented that any book dealing with classics of Texas fiction does not include a discussion of "Noon Wine" or "Old Mortality."

Celia Morris, writing from a feminist perspective,

finds that Katherine Anne Porter is often neglected by her home state:

> Katherine Anne Porter, who grew up here, has been neglected by the official cultural apparatus of our state. McMurtry notes that she suffered from being "genteel to the core," and finds that her best work demonstrates the triumph of the artist in her over the lady . . . Nevertheless, she deserves far more attention than she has gotten in Texas. (114)

"The official cultural apparatus" of the state mentioned by Morris is, presumably, the Texas Institute of Letters.

What must be faced, in this connection, is that only in very recent times has it been to any writer's advantage to be known as a "Texas writer." As late as 1985, as a matter of fact, Clay Reynolds, whose novel, *The Vigil*, had been accepted early that year by a New York publishing house, informed his editor that he "wanted to avoid the stigma of being called a 'Texas writer'" (77). But times have changed. Regional presses have launched successful books dealing with regional characters and settings. The 1986 Sesquicentennial celebrations of the State's founding helped to focus attention on the literature and culture of the State. No longer is it necessary to deny any connections with Texas rednecks in order to succeed as an author. Indeed, the regional presses are on the lookout for good manuscripts dealing with local settings. "Thar's gold in them thar hills," one might say.

Patrick Bennett, in his *Talking with Texas Writers: Twelve Interviews* (1980), displays his exasperation with provincial attitudes toward just who should be considered a "Texas writer." He himself defines a Texas writer as

> one who has spent his formative years in Texas, regardless of where he lives now, or one who has moved to Texas and become a resident. . . . This definition might also include those who moved to Texas, lingered a significant amount of time, and moved on. (6)

Bennett snipingly adds that "Southwestern has nothing to do with it." Nor does subject matter, in his opinion. Such a liberal attitude toward the definition of "Texas writer" would—it is clear—include Katherine Anne Porter.

But when Patrick Bennett asked John Graves which Texas writers he particularly liked, Graves answered:

> Katherine Anne Porter is undoubtedly the most realized artist that has ever come out of

> the state, in terms of literature, but it is hard to
> say whether you should call her a Texas writer.
> Her important stuff has a Texas background to
> it, but she certainly never wanted to identify
> herself with the state particularly. (Bennett
> 85)

Where is it written, one must ask at this point, that
an author can be allowed to determine the critical
categories into which he or she will be judged? That
is the task of literary criticism, not at all the pre-
rogative of the creative writer. Whether or not
Katherine Anne Porter *wanted* to be considered a
Texas writer is an irrelevant question.

"What Does It Take to Be a Texas Writer?" is the
title of Clay Reynolds's 1989 essay that introduces a
great deal of common sense into the question of just
who ought to be classified as a Texas writer:

> . . . to be a Texas writer—or a writer from
> anyplace else—an author has to come to know
> Texas—or that anyplace else—and to respond
> to it with an understanding that goes deeper
> than anything research teams or a quick over-
> view of the land and a few handshakes can ac-
> complish. (81)

That Katherine Anne Porter deserves the title
"Texas writer" as much as James Michener (the im-

plied object of Reynolds's sarcasm) goes without saying.

When one considers the criticism of Graves, Reynolds and McMurtry, certain problems inevitably arise. First, there is the tendency to confuse literature with life. Texas authors have, as Paul Christensen has stated, "a passion for nature and rural life to the exclusion of nearly everything else" (69). The implicit provincialism in this mindset is obvious to everyone who judges Texas literature alongside American or British literature in general. As Kenneth Maclean has said, "the culture made landscape is one of our dominant metaphors" (81). As late as 1988, Jim Corder, a well known rhetorician and writer about all things Texan, states his preferences in this matter very clearly, even daring to utter the dreaded word, *provincialism*:

> I'm not really willing or wanting to *recommend* provincialism; yet I do want to find writers who know, display, and create the province, lifting it in its very ordinariness to its whole accessible meaning . . . I want to find writers of and about this province who will see, marvel at, and praise small things—the ordinary heroes and heroines of our lives, the lonesome landscapes, the sweet, quirky, unhonored people who make the world go, a world full of grace, sadness, lunacy, and joy. (61)

And Texas writers who do not measure up to such standards, presumably, should not be honored by "the official cultural apparatus of the state." Yet an overemphasis upon regional setting or "atmosphere" also has its dangers.

Glen E. Lich, in his splendidly suggestive essay, "Questions about Regional Literature" (1989), argues that those who profess regionalism (those who want to see "regional" texts taught in the schools alongside accepted "classics") ought to be careful how they proceed.

> Those who profess an interest in regional literature—and especially those who wish to include so-called "regional" texts in courses, or who engage in the criticism of regional literature—need to be mindful of an important responsibility in regard to this issue, because discussion which reduces regional literature to plots, sources, and authenticity helps to marginalize regional literature and to trivialize the study of regional literature. (13)

Lich recommends that "regional" texts ought to be studied like any other texts; students ought to be required to handle such matters as "action, plot, setting, characterization, imagery, point of view, structure, language, and style (right down to paragraphing and punctuation), in addition to author-text,

text-reader, and text-context relationships" (12).
What Lich is getting at is clear: regional texts are fit
for the classroom only if they are susceptible of
something more than "authentic setting." They
must have "literary value." But students can be ini-
tially engaged by regional literature because of
their familiarity with the regional setting. A question that teachers might put to young Texas readers,
Lich suggests, goes like this: "whether 'The Jilting
of Granny Weatherall' or *The Vigil* could have happened in Arizona or in Kansas" (13). It is to be hoped
that regionalist students of Porter's "The Jilting of
Granny Weatherall" can come to see its "local" significance as well as its relationships to American
literary culture; the part must somehow be related
to the whole. Regionalism, which many critics continue to think of as "the spatial dimension of plural-
ism" (Lich 14) will cause regional studies to continue an emphasis upon setting, terrain, "local"
culture, and so forth.

Katherine Anne Porter's situation, from this
standpoint, is a bit different from that of a writer
like Clay Reynolds. Clay Reynolds's work is known
in Texas and *ought to be known* nationally; Porter's
reputation is national (even international), but she
ought to be appreciated as a Texas writer. The Texas
regionalist must concern himself with both sides of
this coin.

But Katherine Anne Porter has sometimes not fared well even with sympathetic regionalist critics. As usual, the difficulty involves the pejorative connotations of the concept "regionalism"; the critic fears that a regional tag will obscure the "universal themes" of an author's work. Winfred S. Emmons, in his *Katherine Anne Porter: The Regional Stories* (1967), a brief monograph restricted to the "Texas stories," excluded such narratives as "The Downward Path to Wisdom" and "Rope" from his list, remarking that these stories "might have been set in Texas, but Oregon would have done just as well." Indeed, Emmons went so far as to banish "The Jilting of Granny Weatherall" from the category of Texas fiction on the grounds that "the real setting was in Granny Weatherall's mind" (5). But was it not a *Texas* mind, fenced in with Texas preoccupations? The humiliation of rejection and the fear of death are "universal" themes, of course; but different cultures deal with humiliation and death in diverse ways. By excluding from Texas literature one of the finest short stories written in English in the twentieth century, the regionalist critic has here done no great service to Texas literature. The setting of "Flowering Judas," it might be argued in the same vein, is not Mexico but Laura's mind. But a reader unaware of the Mexican cultural material of that story cannot deal with it in any meaningful

way; neither can a critic ignorant of Texas culture
come to grips with "The Jilting of Granny Weatherall," though no one will deny the "universal" concerns of that remarkable story.

Betsy Colquitt, in "The Landed Heritage of Texas
Writing" (1986), leaves no doubt that she wants
Katherine Anne Porter for Texas letters:

> Despite her ambivalence about her birth-
> place and its literary traditions, both her biog-
> raphy as well as fiction and nonfiction justify
> her being claimed and honored as a Texas
> writer and as the first fiction writer who met
> Dobie's criteria of universality and of art. (179)

And Colquitt goes on to discuss various reasons that
Porter, like some later Texas writers, may not have
felt genuinely comfortable among the Texas literati.

Unfortunately, Katherine Anne Porter herself
was of no great help in these matters. Her numerous
"interviews" were notoriously misleading. In 1963,
when Ray B. West published his University of Minnesota pamphlet, *Katherine Anne Porter*, he was hu-
miliated by Porter's angry denunciation of his work.
Porter pointed out that she *had not* had a Catholic
upbringing, in spite of the fact that on numerous
occasions she *claimed* to have had a Catholic upbringing. West had simply assumed that Katherine
Anne Porter had told the truth in several published

interviews. West's experience taught Porter scholars a lesson they have not forgotten: scholarship
must look beyond the statements of the author.

In addition, Porter's correspondence is erratic in
the matter of her Texas heritage. She publicly renounced the notion of regionalist writers, as in her
1958 interview with Elroy Bode for the *Texas Observer*:

> I don't think we ought to have American
> lyric writers or French provincial writers or
> English country writers . . . I think we ought to
> drop two words: Americanism and regionalism.
> They are coins with the design rubbed off. They
> are cramping people with perfectly good in-
> stincts. Let the artist write what he can. I
> think we should be good writers. (Givner *Con-
> versations* 34)

And that is exactly what Rebecca W. Smith, writing
in the *Saturday Review* in 1942, had to say about
Porter's fiction when she observed that Porter's fiction portrays the Southwest, but "the elusive beauty
of Katherine Anne Porter's art belongs to no section" (13).

It is true that Katherine Anne Porter often
bragged, especially to Texans, that she was the first
and only Texan to have achieved genuine literary
greatness. Writing in 1975 to Professor Roger

Brooks, President of Howard Payne University (the school that was to award her an honorary degree in 1976), she asserted:

> I happen to be the first native of Texas in its whole history to be a professional writer. That is to say, one who had the vocation and practiced only that and lived by and for it all my life. We have had a good many lately in the last quarter of the century perhaps and we have had many people who wrote memoirs and saved many valuable stories and have written immensely interesting and valuable things about Texas; and they are to be valued and understood. But I am very pleased that I am the first who ever was born to the practice of literature. (Qtd. in Givner *KAP* 44)

Scholars of Texas literature and culture will, of course, want to take such comments with the proper dose of salt!

In March of 1975, just five years before her death, Porter published an essay in *The Atlantic*. The eighty-five-year-old author of "Notes on the Texas I Remember" proved herself a writer of fiction to the last; an objective historian she was not. By this time in her life, her literary creations of "the old order" in the South had become—in her own mind—the literal truth, the way things were. Her grandmother, she tells the reader, lived in a six-room house of a style known as Queen Anne:

> It had no features at all except for two long galleries, front and back galleries—mind you, *not* porches or verandas . . . and these galleries were shuttered in green lattice and then covered again with honeysuckle and roses, adding two delightful long summer rooms to the house, the front a dining room, the back furnished with swings and chairs for conversation and repose, iced tea, limeade, sangaree . . . and always, tall frosted beakers of mint julep, for the gentlemen, of course. (102)

The mint julep is a literary touch, of course. And everyone who has read Joan Givner's account of the actual conditions of Porter's life with her grandmother will smile knowingly about the rather luxurious "Southern" embellishments supplied by Porter's vivid imagination. Indeed, Givner, in her essay "Katherine Anne Porter: The Old Order and the New" clearly refutes Porter's wild flights of fancy: "she was raised in a small house (which can still be seen in Kyle south of Austin) in such abject poverty that local people made charitable gifts of clothing to the Porter girls" (58). Even at that late stage in her life, Porter had not come to terms with the appalling poverty of her childhood. It was necessary that she create a Southern upbringing; hence, she had to suppress the *actual* Texas upbringing.

But, as was usually the case with Porter, the essay was revealing of what life had finally made her. Speaking of the days of her childhood in South Texas, she mentions the riffraff of that period:

> Not long ago, I saw a photograph of a whole row of dead bandits of that era, all laid out orderly in their working clothes, looking very helpless and unkempt and homeless in a barn or kind of shed and with a touchingly indifferent stare in their open eyes; this is what I remember from just a quick glimpse, turning the page in a hurry, but the impression has stayed by me of something pitiable, mysteriously innocent, somehow wronged and wasted—all the soft-headed western Christian sentiments I was brought up on, in short. And seeing what this sort of thing can lead to, I fight it furiously in myself. For I have seen how insidiously our natures will work almost unconsciously in defense of the killer rather than his victim. How at last we can persuade ourselves that the victim, not the killer, was really in the deepest sense the guilty one. . . . I can always rule my misguided sympathies by remembering how the men they murdered looked—much the same, no doubt—and how their families and friends looked, and just what it was like for

them; and I am still able to draw that fine hair-
line between justice and revenge. (106)

Whether or not Porter had ever seen such a photograph does not really matter; in fact, such a scene as
she describes is more likely a memory of events in
Mexico. But what rings true is her reference to "all
the soft-headed western Christian sentiments I was
brought up on" and her later spurning of such mush.
This sentiment is as Texan as a chicken-fried steak.

It is unfortunate, of course, that what has passed
for literary criticism in Texas, at least as regards
Katherine Anne Porter as a Texas writer, has placed
undue emphasis upon what the author herself has
said, as if the critic ought to believe everything he or
she hears from an author. It goes without saying
that most Texans swallowed—hook, line, and
sinker—most of the self-serving misinformation put
out by Katherine Anne Porter for the public. To take
just two examples from among many possible, Ruthe
Winegarten, in the popular reference work, *Texas
Women: A Pictorial History* (1985), includes this en-
try for Katherine Anne Porter:

> *Katherine Anne Porter* (1892–1980). Kather-
> ine Anne Porter wrote her first novel at the age
> of six and her second at the age of seventy-
> one—*Ship of Fools*. It earned her $1 million
> and the Pulitzer Prize and was made into a

> movie with Vivien Leigh and Lee Marvin. She
> left Texas at the age of eighteen because, "I
> didn't want to be regarded as a freak; that was
> how they regarded women who tried to write. I
> had to make a revolt, a rebellion." (80)

One would certainly like to know the title of the
novel written by the six-year-old Katherine Anne
Porter! And, as usual, the date of birth is wrong by
two years, an inexcusable error coming three years
after Givner's biography had corrected Porter's fal-
sification of her age. Furthermore, Porter's absurd
statement that women who tried to write were regarded as freaks is accepted without the slightest
objection or further explanation.

And we are no better served by Edward Simmen
in the Introduction to his anthology, *Gringos in
Mexico* (1988). Simmen tells us that Katherine Anne
Porter visited Mexico "as a girl of ten . . . with her
father in 1900—only five years after Crane and several years before Flandrau, Reed and London"
(xxxvi). The fact that Simmen relied on statements
from Porter's own interviews is no excuse. Again,
Givner's 1982 biography clearly establishes the fact
that Katherine Anne Porter first visited Mexico in
1920, a full decade later than Simmen would have it.

While these two examples might be thought of as
minor misdemeanors, they clearly establish the utter unreliability of Porter as a witness in her own

case. But what is worse, critics tend—for some unfathomable reason—to take to heart her own pro-
nouncements on her artistic intentions as if they
were somehow to be considered more trustworthy
than her biographical falsifications. And Texas critics seem most gullible.

It may be that the judges for the Texas Institute of
Letters paid too much attention to Porter's published interviews and too little to the texts of Porter's fiction in 1939. Joan Givner describes Porter's
deep disappointment over the actions of the Texas
Institute of Letters:

> In 1939, the Texas Institute of Letters,
> founded in 1936 for "The Promotion and Rec-
> ognition of Literature in Texas," announced its
> first award for the best book by a Texas writer.
> *Pale Horse, Pale Rider* had been in the running
> and seemed a certain winner, since no other
> author had achieved Porter's national stature.
> When she learned that the prize had gone to J.
> Frank Dobie for *Apache Gold and Yaqui Silver*
> because of the "indigenous nature" of his sub-
> ject matter and because he was not only a na-
> tive but had remained in Texas, she was con-
> vinced once again that Texas was no place for
> her. (*KAP* 315)

If one were to take the announced criteria of the
Texas Institute of Letters seriously (and no one re-

ally did, or does), the genuine Texas writer ought to
have been born in Texas, to have written about
purely Texas subjects, and to have *stayed* in Texas. It is clear, that neither Larry McMurtry nor
Donald Barthelme in later times would be able to
meet such criteria. And Joan Givner, writing from a
feminist viewpoint, believes that Dobie really won
the award because of his assertively masculine
style:

> I think he [Dobie] would have won out over
> Jane Austen, Jean Rhys, Eudora Welty, Mari-
> anne Moore, Virginia Woolf, and the entire
> Bronte clan all lumped together. And he would
> have done so even if these writers had been
> born in Waco, lived all their lives in Waco, and
> died in Waco. ("The Old Order and the New"
> 60)

Most people today would agree that Porter's *Pale
Horse, Pale Rider* is of considerably greater literary
value that Dobie's *Apachi Gold and Yaqui Silver*.
There is considerable unintended irony, therefore,
in Dobie's 1939 letter to Tom Lea, the gifted illus-
trator of *Apachi Gold and Yaqui Silver*. Dobie
praised Lea's pictures in the very way that serious
critics were praising Katherine Anne Porter's fiction:

> These pictures are the expression of a man who understands a vast land peculiar unto itself, a land with a culture of its own that he burns to reveal and make the dwellers in that land understand as their own inheritance. The only art and literature worth an Indian fig that the Southwest will ever have will be art and literature growing out of the Southwest's own rocks and soil, burned by its own suns, sifted by its own winds, given perspective by its own spaces, and humanized and dramatized in the personalities that have made up its own population—people who belong, like Tom Lea, to the land. (Hjerter x)

It would be difficult to conceive of any better way of describing "Noon Wine."

When, in 1962, the Texas Institute of Letters finally gave Porter its prize for the best book of fiction (for *Ship of Fools*), it clearly revealed its lack of any objective standards. For one thing, *Ship of Fools* is—for practically all readers—tedious beyond endurance, a failure as a work of fiction. It deserved no prize, from the Texas Institute of Letters or from anybody else. And the fact that the book won a Pulitzer prize is no defense. *Pale Horse, Pale Rider* was a book worthy of many prizes; *Ship of Fools* was launched on hoopla.

Suffice it to say, that before all was said and done, the Texas Institute of Letters needed Katherine Anne Porter more than Katherine Anne Porter needed the Texas Institute of Letters. But it is quite clear that she was deeply hurt by the Institute's apparent rejection of her work. Furthermore, it seems clear that she ascribed similar attitudes toward the citizens of Texas generally—this despite the fact that the ordinary citizens of Texas were scarcely aware even of the existence of the Texas Institute of Letters.

Porter's contempt for the Texas Institute of Letters and for other Texas cultural organizations is at least partly justified. But we must be fair. The Institute was established to promote "Texas literature," and Katherine Anne Porter wrote about much besides things Texan (though the "Texas" content tends to be underestimated).

The real argument of Texas regionalists is that a Texas storyteller should not subordinate "the local and the immediate" in order to elevate "the timeless and universal." The true regionalist believes, like dedicated adherents of realism generally, that the local and immediate *is*, viewed rightly, the timeless and universal; that only through an absorption in the landscape and daily life of the region is a truly "universal" and "timeless" depiction of human experience possible. Aside from the commonsense objection that critics have no business dictating subject matter to authors, and one author certainly has no business requiring prefabricated subject matter for another author, such a position can lead to provincialism. The danger is that a great writer may emerge who transmutes, symbolizes, interprets the landscape and the daily existence of the region, but who does not, in the ordinary sense, produce an "indigenous" work. Most critics will agree that an author's upbringing, education, and early experiences in any given "place" cannot be erased from his consciousness, nor can they be utterly absent in his artistic productions, disguised though they may be. What is disturbing about run-of-the-mill regionalists is that they so often invoke hifalutin phrases like "the sense of place" in such pitifully narrow contexts. For Texas regionalists, nature and rural life seem to be requisite; so that a Texas writer who depicts life in the great cities, or who deigns to describe the inner workings of human consciousness, risks censure. A Katherine Anne Porter or a Donald Barthelme cannot really meet such narrow, rigid criteria. Yet they are both, in a very real sense, "Texas writers."

The sympathetic regionalist critic ought to allow Texas writers at least some strategic leeway in making themselves heard in the outlands beyond Texas. A variety of strategies probably will be necessary for any regional writer to appeal to a more national audience. Even as late as 1968, Larry McMurtry felt bound to say that "As a regionalist, and a regionalist from an unpopular region, I find the problem of how to get heard rather a fascinating problem" (*In a Narrow Grave* xviii). And McMurtry's various strategies, like those of Katherine Anne Porter, to cope with this problem, make for a fascinating study in literary history.

Anyone interested in the general subject of literary regionalism, and Texas regionalism in particular, should read Don Graham's delightful essay, "Some Thoughts on Regionalism," the Afterword in his *Texas: A Literary Portrait* (1985), as well as William A. Owens's "Regionalism and Universality" in *The Texas Literary Tradition* (1983).

Another objection raised against Katherine Anne Porter as a Texas writer is that she is somehow "Southern" in a state seen by many as "Southwestern" or "Western," with the term "Southern" meaning—in this critical context—genteel, mealy-mouthed, nostalgic, obsolete, and respectable. Porter's early stories set in Texas seem, to some critics, to emphasize the "Southern" side of Texas rather than its "Southwestern" essence. But a close reading of the Texas stories will not bear out such an opinion. Indeed, there are stories that pervasively condemn gentility and "respectability" (*Noon Wine* comes to mind). On the other hand, historians of Texas literature and culture remind us that Texas *did* fight on the side of the South in the Civil War, that Texas *was* a slaveholding state, that many settlers in Texas came from the deep South after the end of the Civil War, and that the vestiges of slavery and segregation are indeed still with us. Still, the "Southern" side of Texas culture seems more easily forgettable to modern Texans than the "Southwestern" or "Western" side. And since Katherine Anne Porter was not really into cattle drives, ranching, train robberies, and oil wells, she seems somehow not to fit in with the Texas described by J. Frank Dobie and the "Western" school of Texas culturists. (In this connection, it is interesting to note that Paul Christensen, perhaps the foremost authority on Texas poetry, has found it necessary to describe, in his essay, "Allowing for Such Talk," the "Southwestern" elements even in the work of Vassar Miller, a religious mystical poet who at first glance would seem to have little in common with "Southwestern" literature.)

It does seem that the marketers of Porter's fiction found that it was in their interest to describe her as a "Southern" writer rather than as a "Texas" or "Southwestern" writer. It must be remembered, after all, that the South was experiencing something of a boom in art and letters during this period. An

example of such marketing is easy to cite—the blurb
on the book jacket designed by Harcourt, Brace for
Porter's *Collected Stories* when the volume appeared
in 1965:

> Cyril Connoly, writing of this new volume in
> the London *Sunday Times*, says, "This is an
> original talent, a sensitive Southern writer
> who stands in time somewhere between Willa
> Cather and the Carson McCullers/Eudora
> Welty group, with something of Faulkner's un-
> derstanding of the Southern petit bourgeoisie
> and also his ribald sense of fun. (*Collected Sto-
> ries*, 1965, book jacket)

The prospective reader is thus led to believe that
Katherine Anne Porter partakes of a great Southern
tradition and is to be thought of in the same company as Faulkner and Cather and Welty, excellent
company indeed.

James W. Lee believes that Katherine Anne Porter, "making some allowances for distortion," followed "the Southern tradition" in Texas writing, the
tradition, he argues, that most Texans knew in the
first half of the twentieth century (48). "Some distortion" there certainly is, for it is clear that Katherine Anne Porter deliberately defamiliarized her
early Texas upbringing in order to deal with it creatively. One hopes that creative writers will be al-

lowed to "distort" (one ought, perhaps, to use the more correct "defamiliarize" to avoid a moralistic or pejorative slant) whatever they please so long as imaginative truth is maintained. Psychological realism (the type of fiction Porter was attempting to write) will not always accord with realism in the ordinary sense, as Henry James long ago pointed out. Porter's stories in *The Old Order*, describing the Plantation South, good-natured darkies, and all the rest of the stereotypical Southern landscape cannot really be judged on the basis of regional realism; their effectiveness is proof that aesthetic success has been achieved, whatever the ideology that may have been violated.

Yet it must be observed that narratives like "Noon Wine" (1936) hardly partake at all of what is normally thought of as "the Southern tradition" in Texas writing. Furthermore, Porter's characters, for the most part, are not stereotypically "Southern." Winfred Emmons observes, indeed, that "None of her characters, except her Negroes, are so Southern as to be incapable of living almost anywhere" (1). Neither does such a work owe anything to what has come to be thought of as the "Western" tradition. Owing much to Sherwood Anderson's *Winesburg, Ohio* (1919) and other psychological realism of the early twentieth century, such a story concerns itself far more with the truths of human consciousness

than with objectively correct descriptions of landscape; yet the landscape has penetrated into the
troubled consciousness of all the characters, and the
"sense of place" is by no means absent in this and
similar works.

That the "Western" mindset of critics of Texas culture has adverse literary effects has already been
seen in the damning observations of Larry Mc-
Murtry and others. But Texas is a big place; there is
room for great diversity in its literature.

Why did Katherine Anne Porter seek to distance
herself from Texas? First, at the time that Porter
first maneuvered for prominence in American letters (the 1920s) being identified as a Texas writer, or
a regional writer of any kind for that matter, would
not have been helpful. Second, Porter was a miniaturist, primarily a first-rate writer of short stories;
her hope of establishing a reputation as a short story
writer lay with her cultivation of editors and pub-
lishers of sophisticated Northern periodicals. As a
"Texas writer" she would have had to produce a
full-length novel occasionally to keep her name before the regional audience. Third, for Porter herself, being identified as a Texas writer would have
been somewhat humiliating. A fiercely competitive
writer, she longed for vindication of her talent on
the national and even international stage. For a person of Porter's temperament, the mere suggestion of

provincialism would have been lethal. Her intense motivation to transcend her difficult childhood and upbringing in Texas, and her inner fear that she would not in the end accomplish her purposes, made it necessary for her to deny her Texas origins. Fourth, Katherine Anne Porter was a woman. And it was difficult for a woman, at that time, to establish herself in Texas letters. Women had an easier time, creatively, working in New York or Mexico or Europe—the places where Porter actually spent most of her time rather than in Texas. The case of Dorothy Scarborough's *The Wind* (1925) might be cited as a case in point.

A distinctively feminist bias, though it has yet to be exhaustively treated by literary criticism, is undeniably present in Katherine Anne Porter's fiction. It may be that Texas simply was not the place for a woman of Porter's talents to be during the period of her greatest productivity, the 1920s and 1930s. Larry McMurtry, in his essay "Eros in Archer County," describes the predicament of women like Porter:

> The pioneer [Texas] woman had to cope with deprivation and physical hardship, but I am not sure but what the women who came to maturity in Texas in the twenties and thirties were even worse off. They had to cope, not with raw nature, but with a new and difficult con-

> cept of womanhood, one for which nothing in
> their early training had prepared them. They
> suddenly found themselves expected to be the
> equals of men, not merely socially and politi-
> cally, but sexually as well. (*In a Narrow Grave*
> 68–69)

But it is clear that Texas husbands, and Texas men
in general, were not yet ready to accommodate the
new woman. Katherine Anne Porter was no doubt
wise to absent herself from such an infelicitous environment. One can see evidence of sexual terror
and sexual repression in stories such as "The Grave"
and "The Downward Path to Wisdom," owing a
great deal to Porter's Texas upbringing.

In spite of Katherine Anne Porter's disavowal of
her own Texas origins, she nevertheless has influenced subsequent Texas writers. Indeed, a scholarly
volume needs to be written detailing this important
influence. For example, Joan Givner, in her splendid essay, "Katherine Anne Porter: The Old Order
and the New," written for *The Texas Literary Tradition*, points especially to Porter's profound influence upon William Humphrey and William Goyen,
mainly in matters of style. Both these men, according to Givner, were aesthetes "drawn to the lyrical,
elegant androgynous style which has always been
associated with the aesthete." And they, like Porter,
were either ignored or underestimated in Texas let-

ters because of Texans' tendency to undervalue the aesthetic writer. Givner remarks that it must have been "very reassuring . . . for Goyen, when he was ignored in Texas, to know that so also was Katherine Anne Porter" (64). When Goyen's first book, *House of Breath*, was published in 1950, he wrote in her presentation copy that it had been written "with her and her great work as his guiding light" (Givner *KAP* 377). Porter's influence on these two important Texas writers is easily documented because of the extensive correspondence that has survived between Porter and the two men, not that anyone would be inclined to dispute it. The fact that Goyen was briefly the lover of Katherine Anne Porter makes the literary relationship all the more interesting.

Porter once responded, when told of Thomas Wolfe's opinion that "you can't go home again," with the curt "Nonsense, it's the only place you can go" (*Conversations* 189). Born in Indian Creek, Texas, in 1890, she was always a "Texas writer," even though she roamed widely, and though she seems, to some readers and critics, to represent a more "Southern" and genteel aspect of Texas than they would like to have represented in literature. Though she did not live permanently in Texas and did not often visit, her stories are preoccupied with Texas settings and Texas characters. A. C. Greene was perfectly correct; many of her best stories have a Texas background.

Most revealing of all, when she chose her own burial site, she chose to be buried beside her mother in the little cemetery at Indian Creek, Texas.

Katherine Anne Porter is the greatest writer yet produced by Texas. Yet she is scarcely acknowledged as a Texas writer at all. No Katherine Anne Porter Society in Texas attempts to celebrate her work or keep her name alive. No Texas library attempts in any systematic way to collect her manuscripts or memorabilia. No memorial society cares for her gravesite in Indian Creek, Texas. Misunderstood as a "Southern" writer by critics too prone to take her at her word, she continues to be anthologized in American literature collections, yet largely neglected in her home state.

2

"A LITTLE GIRL FROM TEXAS": THE LIFE OF KATHERINE ANNE PORTER

"I was just a little girl from Texas in New York." (Katherine Anne Porter to Winston Bode, in a 1958 interview for the *Texas Observer*)

Several obsessive themes inform the fiction of Katherine Anne Porter, reflecting the compulsive preoccupations of the author. Repeatedly we find in her narratives: (1) a passive, ineffectual male unable to cope with domestic responsibilities ("That Tree," "Rope," "A Day's Work"); (2) a dominant, take-charge female imposing order in domestic chaos ("María Concepción," "The Source," "A Day's Work"); (3) a defective child or helpless individual in a hostile environment ("He," "Holiday," "The Downward Path to Wisdom," Herr Glocken in *Ship of Fools*); (4) the passive advancement and encouragement of evil by ostensibly "innocent" or "respectable" people ("Flowering Judas," "Magic," "The Leaning Tower," *Noon Wine*); and betrayal of trust in many forms ("Flowering Judas," "Theft"). All these compulsive preoccupations in thematic mate-

rial were the result of Porter's early life in Texas.
Givner's biography repeatedly documents such concerns in Porter's career.

Katherine Anne Porter (originally Callie Russell
Porter) was born in a log cabin on May 15, 1890 in
Indian Creek, Texas, near Brownwood, in Brown
County. She was the fourth of five children of Harrison Boone Porter and Mary Alice Jones Porter.
Because both her parents were Methodist, she was
baptized in the Methodist Church. In 1892, when
Katherine Anne Porter was only two years old, her
mother died, leaving the family in desperate circumstances. The family then moved to Kyle, Texas, in
Hays County, where Harrison Porter's mother,
Catherine Anne Skaggs Porter (Aunt Cat) took
them in. Harrison Porter was devastated by his
wife's death, and thereafter remained passive, ineffectual, and melancholy; he became, in Katherine
Anne Porter's fiction, the model for the ineffectual,
whining, can't-do male. Despite overwhelming poverty and deprivation, Aunt Cat managed, by sheer
determination and Calvinistic willpower, to raise
her son's family. This paternal grandmother was to
be the model for many of Katherine Anne Porter's
resourceful, indomitable, and intimidating heroines.

In 1901, when Katherine Anne Porter was eleven
years old, her grandmother died. Her grandmother's

death precipitated a period of indecision and vague longing, according to her biographer, Joan Givner. Subsequently, the family lived in San Antonio where Porter attended the Thomas School, a nonsectarian boarding school. It was at this period of her life that Porter conceived the desire to be an actress, performing in several summer stock productions. Throughout her subsequent life, Porter was often accused of "performing" for special effects. After leaving school, she taught classes in music and dramatic reading in Victoria, Texas.

In 1906, Porter, now only sixteen years old, married John Henry Koontz of Inez, Texas. Koontz, a clerk on the Southern Pacific Railway, came from a prosperous farm family of Swiss descent. The marriage was unfortunate, though it lasted nine years and was the means by which Porter escaped the narrow confines of her childhood world. Koontz's family was Roman Catholic, and in 1908 Porter converted to that faith, in which she remained for the rest of her life, though just how serious her theological convictions were is open to considerable debate (the aesthetic and cultural connotations of the Roman Catholic faith seeming, for some, to be the primary attraction for Porter). In 1914, Porter simply fled the marriage and left for Chicago to work in the motion pictures, finally divorcing Koontz in 1915, the same year that she became seriously ill with tuberculosis brought on by mental and physical strain.

During her period of convalescence in 1916, she ran an outdoor school in Dallas, Texas, for tubercular children. After a period of confinement in tuberculosis sanatoriums, she was employed in 1917 (to cover theatrical and social events) by the *Fort Worth Critic*. In 1918–19, she worked for the *Rocky Mountain News* in Denver, where she became a popular reviewer of books and theatrical performances. During this period, she came close to death in the influenza epidemic that engulfed the nation at the close of World War I. This brush with death later became the setting for her short novel, *Pale Horse, Pale Rider*, and the valuable journalistic experience that she had gained in both Texas and Colorado came into play in this work.

In 1919–20, Porter worked in New York as a publicist for a motion picture company; she ghost-wrote a novel; and she published stories in the children's magazine *Everyland* and elsewhere. It was in New York in 1919 that she was introduced to several expatriate Mexican artists who helped her to make connections with magazines interested in publishing journalistic works on Mexico. She eagerly took advantage of this opportunity.

Porter's first visit to Mexico came in 1920, and she

arrived there while the Obregón Revolution was still in progress. During the years 1921–1930, she lived mainly in the eastern United States but made frequent visits to Mexico. Poetry, book reviews, and short stories began to appear. Beginning in 1921, and continuing over many years, Porter wrote a number of insightful analytical essays dealing with Mexico and its problems. But in that same year she was forced to leave Mexico, and she returned to Fort Worth for a few months.

In 1922, she returned to New York. In was in this year that she published "María Concepción," her first serious attempt in the short story form, in *Century Magazine*; this was the beginning of her distinguished career in short fiction. The story was set in Mexico, a nation Porter was getting to know better all the time. As an "authority" on life south of the border, Porter was now in a position to solicit various journalistic work relating to Mexico. The 1922 visit to Mexico was for the purpose of writing a catalogue for an exhibition of Mexican folk-art, an exhibition that, unfortunately, did not prosper.

Porter continued to publish distinguished short stories, "The Martyr" appearing in 1923, and "Virgin Violeta" in 1924, both stories with Mexican settings.

In 1925–1926, there was a brief, unsatisfactory marriage to Ernest Stock, an English World War I

pilot. Stock was a charming rake, passive in temperament, who exasperated Porter. His type is represented in numerous Porter short stories.

During the fall and winter of 1927–28, Porter
lived in Salem, Massachusetts, where she was attempting to continue her research for a biography of
Cotton Mather, a work that she was never able to
complete. While in the atmosphere of Salem, she
gradually came under the spell of Nathaniel Hawthorne and his romances of moral ambiguity and
hereditary determinism. And it was in Salem that
Porter completed at least two short stories that partake of Hawthornian qualities—"Magic," and "The
Jilting of Granny Weatherall."

In 1927, she became absorbed in the Sacco and
Vanzetti case, allowing herself to be arrested on
more than one occasion. It was not, however, until
many years later (1977) that she published an account of this famous case. It may be that the short
story "He," published in this same year, suggests a
sense of injustice growing out of this torturous experience.

In 1929, "Magic" and "Rope" appeared in print. It
was in this year also that she spent five months in
Bermuda in a futile effort to finish *The Devil and
Cotton Mather*. But it was during this idyllic period
that she conceived the ideas for the stories eventually known as "The Old Order" and "Old Mortality,"

both with Texas settings. "The Jilting of Granny Weatherall," with its marvelous portrait of her Grandmother (Aunt Cat) Porter, and "Theft," with its Hawthornesque ambiguity commingling villain and victim, were published in this same year. And "The Fig Tree" was actually completed in Bermuda in 1929, but the story was not published until June of 1960 when it appeared in *Harper's Magazine.* More important than anything else about this Bermuda experience, however, was that it supplied the imaginative Southern setting for her stories of the Texas South. The plantation atmosphere of *The Old Order* stories owed nothing to Porter's actual upbringing, but instead to the ancestral Hilgrove estate in Bermuda, as has been massively documented in Givner's biography.

In 1930, after her return to the United States, came publication of "Flowering Judas," considered by many to be her most successful story, and the work that established her reputation. The 1930s were to be her most productive period. It was in 1930 also that she began her longest period of residence in Mexico. There she met Eugene Pressly with whom she spent the next six years. Pressly was at that time employed by the Crane Foundation in Mexico City. She spent two days on the set of Eisenstein's abortive movie, *Que Viva Mexico,* which she was later to describe in "Hacienda." In 1931 she sailed,

accompanied by Pressly, from Veracruz, Mexico, to
Bremerhaven, Germany, on board the German ship
S.S. *Werra*. She lived alone in Berlin the fall of 1931.
Her observations during this voyage, and the subsequent months in which she lived in Berlin during
the period of Hitler's rise to power, eventually came
to fruition in "The Leaning Tower," set in the Berlin
of 1931, but not published until 1941, and much of
the content of *Ship of Fools* (1962). While in Berlin,
Porter was escorted on at least one occasion by Her-
man Goering, but not, as she led some to believe, by
Adolph Hitler. The "Texas characters" in both "The
Leaning Tower" and *Ship of Fools* show that her
native state was never far from her imagination.

In 1932, still in Europe and still connected with
Eugene Pressly, she visited Madrid, Paris, and
Basel, cities where Pressly was employed by the
American Embassy. "The Cracked Looking-Glass,"
reflective of her relationship with Pressly, was published. The early version of "Hacienda" appeared in
1932, though it was extensively revised in 1934.

In 1933 she settled in Paris and married Eugene
Pressly. Despite the difficulties she encountered in
living with Pressly, he was of great assistance to her
career. A career diplomat, he was at the time a lowly
secretarial assistant. Although passive and indecisive (like her father), he was intensely loyal, a "one-
woman man" (again, like her father). While in

France, she translated an old *French Song Book* (1933). It was while she was in France that she began to understand the value of investigating her roots. To escape from Pressly, who—she thought— interfered with her creative work—she left France and returned to Texas for the first time in fifteen years. While on this visit, she attempted to piece together the family life of her relatives.

In 1934, Porter published "That Tree" as well as the revised version of "Hacienda." These stories were followed, in 1935, by "The Circus" and "The Grave." In 1936, Porter returned to America. She spent a productive writing period in Doylestown, Pennsylvania, finishing "Noon Wine" and "Old Mortality", and beginning work on "Pale Horse, Pale Rider." "The Old Order" (later re-titled "The Journey") and "Noon Wine" were published.

In 1937, separated from Eugene Pressly, she went to New Orleans and began a relationship with Albert Erskine, a young Ph.D. student who worked as business manager for *The Southern Review* under Cleanth Brooks. Porter and Erskine were married in April of 1938, with Robert Penn Warren and his wife as witnesses to the ceremony. Erskine was twenty-seven years old, and Katherine Anne Porter was forty-eight. Erskine had been led to believe that she was much younger. Joan Givner reports the mortifying marriage scene:

> [Erskine] had thought she was approaching forty, and when he found out, during the marriage ceremony, that she was nearly fifty, he was horrified. This was a moment of the deepest humiliation for her and she never quite got over it. (*KAP* 311)

Porter must have felt a bit like Granny Weatherall, the heroine of her 1929 story, "The Jilting of Granny Weatherall." In a sense, Erskine's reaction was a betrayal, rejection, or "jilting" of her at the beginning of the marriage. To make matters worse, Porter and Erskine were frequently mistaken for mother and son. Unable to work in Erskine's presence, she spent the winter of 1938 writing in Houston, Texas. Though she was despondent, the year 1938 was creatively significant, since it saw the publication of "Pale Horse, Pale Rider" and "Old Mortality," two of her most enduring works. By the spring of 1940, Erskine and Porter agreed that they could no longer live together and effected a separation, though they were not legally divorced until 1942. The marriage had been a total disaster for both partners.

In 1939 came publication of "The Downward Path to Wisdom," an intriguing quasi-theological depiction of original sin. But more important, this was the year of the book-length collection of three short novels, entitled *Pale Horse, Pale Rider* (dedicated, surprisingly, to her Texas father, Harrison Boone Porter), a collection of three short novels ("Pale Horse, Pale Rider," "Old Mortality," and "Noon Wine") . Porter had hoped, indeed expected, that the Texas Institute of Letters would give its award for the best Texas book of 1939 to *Pale Horse, Pale Rider*. When, instead, J. Frank Dobie won the award for *Apachi Gold and Yaqui Silver*, she was bitterly disappointed. She really never forgave the Texas Institute of Letters for what was, to her, an insult.

When Porter and Albert Erskine separated in 1940, she decided to relocate to the artist colony at Yaddo, in upstate New York. Later, she settled into a home of her own in Saratoga Springs, New York. "A Day's Work," describing life among the poor Irish in New York, was published in that same year. It was apparently in 1940 that she began work on what was eventually to become *Ship of Fools*.

"The Leaning Tower" and "The Source" appeared in 1941. In 1942, Porter published *The Itching Parrot*, a translation of José Joaquín Fernandez de Lizárdi's *El Perequillo Sarniento*, a work that had been finished long before. Actually this was a complete rewriting of the novel in English. Eugene Pressly, an excellent linguist, had really done most of the translation from the Spanish (Givner *KAP* 340). For this translation, Porter wrote a lengthy introduction. It was in 1942, also, that Katherine Anne Porter's father died. She was emotionally affected by his death, but she did not attend the funeral.

In 1944, she published *The Leaning Tower and Other Stories*. "The Last Leaf" appeared in 1944, as did "The Witness."

In 1945, finding herself unable to complete the manuscript of *Ship of Fools*, suffering from what she considered intolerable loneliness, and in considerable financial difficulty, she put in brief stints as a Hollywood scriptwriter and stayed on in California for a time, even after such work proved not to her liking.

Beginning in 1948, Katherine Anne Porter began accepting lecture tours as well as teaching appointments in various universities. In 1948–49 she taught at Stanford and afterwards returned to New York to live. In the winter of 1951, while living at Yaddo, she and William Goyen, the Texas novelist, became lovers for a brief period (Givner *KAP* 377). In 1954 she published *The Days Before*, a collection of essays (later to be incorporated into her *Collected Essays and Occasional Writings*). In 1953–54, she taught at the University of Michigan. Later, she taught at Liège and at Washington and Lee.

In 1954, her Fulbright lectureship at the University of Liège was terminated by illness. She returned to the United States and lived in Connecticut.

In the fall of 1958, Katherine Anne Porter was swollen with pride because of rumors that Harry Ransom, who was responsible for creating and maintaining the Humanities Research Center at the University of Texas, wanted to name a building in her honor. Supposedly, this was a top-secret plan that would be announced at the appropriate time. Porter was so enthusiastic upon hearing these rumors that she actually planned to settle near Austin to be near her library and to donate her papers to the University of Texas at Austin. It is not clear just how much truth there was in the rumors that she took so seriously. But it is very clear that when no building, or room in any library, was named for her, she was once again bitterly disappointed in Texas.

Nevertheless, at the time Porter was invited to lecture at the University in the fall of 1958, she was in top spirits, still believing that the University of Texas was to honor her and provide a place for her collected papers. While in Austin, she was interviewed by Winston Bode for the *Texas Observer*; his interview, titled "Miss Porter on Writers and Writing," brought her once again to the attention of her fellow Texans. The wife of William Handy, a faculty member at the University of Texas, had written a

master's thesis on Porter (which Porter did not read
until after she had left Austin, and which infuriated
her when she did read it), and it was the Handys
who showed Porter around during her stay in Austin
(Givner *KAP* 424, 426–27).

To make matters worse, Porter became infuriated
that the *Texas Quarterly* allowed her subscription to
lapse, and Austin real estate dealers hounded her,
trying to sell her high-priced housing instead of the
type of housing she was interested in. All in all, the
Texas trip was a fiasco.

In 1959, well supported now by the Ford Foundation, and wishing to finish *Ship of Fools*, she settled
in the Washington, D.C., area, near the McKeldin
Library of the University of Maryland, which eventually was to house her private papers and manuscripts.

"The Fig Tree" and "Holiday" (both written many
years earlier) were published in 1960.

In 1962, *Ship of Fools* finally appeared. A great
popular success at the time, and the basis of a popular motion picture with many famous actors, this
work—her only full-length novel—has not demonstrated staying power. At any rate, the financial returns from this book finally gave Katherine Anne
Porter the economic security for which she had long
yearned. And the receipt of the Texas Institute of
Letters award for the best piece of fiction, in addi-

tion to the Pulitzer Prize, satisfied her desire for both national and regional recognition.

In 1965, she published *The Collected Stories of Katherine Anne Porter*, for which she was awarded, in 1966, both the Pulitzer Prize and the National Book Award. Honorary degrees were adding up by this time, but Porter hungered for more. She received honorary doctorates from the University of North Carolina at Greensboro, Smith College, Wheaton College, the University of Michigan, and from LaSalle College, as well as others. By this time also, she had been a vice president of the National Institute of Arts and Letters and a Fellow of Regional American Literature in the Library of Congress; she had received two Guggenheim Fellowships and a Ford Foundation grant and was awarded the gold medal of the Society for the Libraries of New York University. She was in demand everywhere as a lecturer and prospective adjunct professor.

In 1967, the Katherine Anne Porter Room at the University of Maryland Library was established, housing her manuscripts, letters, books, miscellaneous papers, and personal memorabilia.

In 1970, *The Collected Essays and Occasional Writings of Katherine Anne Porter*, covering a span of nearly fifty years, was published. These essays show Katherine Anne Porter to have been a wide and discriminating reader. Her opinions are impressionistic but stoutly maintained. Students of her literary criticism will find this collection a happy hunting ground of witty aphorisms dealing with the Hebrew prophets, the Greek dramatists, Goethe, Dante, Shakespeare, Tolstoy, Flaubert, Joyce, Pound, Edith Sitwell, D. H. Lawrence, Thomas Hardy, Jacqueline Kennedy, Flannery O'Connor, Gertrude Stein, Virginia Woolf, and many others. Porter is here revealed as a genuine woman of letters, highly educated in her craft, astutely aware of what she was about. Essays dealing with communism in Hollywood, Mexican culture, the Dylan Thomas legend, and writing technique—all these show her wide-ranging interests. The charming "conversational" style of her essays is especially enjoyable. Here one even finds Porter's early poems, and one understands why she renounced poetry in favor of short fiction. The volume is a fascinating one; and, if used with the usual proper cautions, is of great value in the study of Katherine Anne Porter's life and works.

By 1973, she was becoming senile. M. M. Liberman's essay, "Meeting Miss Porter," describes a meeting with Porter in that year and being asked to be her literary trustee, then dropped quickly for no apparent reason, amid chaos in the household. In spite of everything, Liberman refers to her as "the nation's most accomplished writer of short fiction" (300). Her essay, "Notes on the Texas I Remember," appeared in *The Atlantic* for March of 1975. It is interesting to note that this essay was not included in her *Collected Essays and Occasional Writings*. As usual, Porter's memories of Texas are conflated with other scenes and memories. Even at this late date, Porter was unable to face the reality of the devastating poverty in which she had been raised.

In the spring semester of 1976, Howard Payne University in Brownwood, Texas, located near Katherine Anne Porter's Indian Creek birthplace, conducted a course dealing with her literary works. At the conclusion of the course, the University scheduled a conference to which were invited Porter scholars from throughout the United States and Canada. The culmination of this event was the awarding of an honorary degree to Katherine Anne Porter on May 7, 1976. The eighty-six year old Porter, in extremely frail health, was deeply touched by these events. The next day was May 8, the exact day, as Givner points out, "when in 1936 she had returned from Paris and visited the cemetery" (*KAP* 502). On this day she returned to the little cemetery at Indian Creek to view the grave of her mother. It was at this time that Porter apparently shook off any surviving ill will toward her native state. As her biographer says, "Feeling that she had at last made

her reconciliation with Texas, she decided that when
she died she would have her body brought back to
the Indian Creek cemetery to lie beside her mother's" (Givner *KAP* 502).

Later in 1976, after considerable traveling and
lecturing, she was left bedridden by a series of
strokes.

In 1977, she published *The Never-Ending Wrong*,
her last book, an account of her experiences during
the last days of Sacco and Vanzetti in 1927. This
book appeared soon after she had been stricken by
the strokes.

She died in 1980, and is buried beside her mother
in the Indian Creek cemetery.

As is well known, Katherine Anne Porter frequently misled others about the facts of her life. Apparently, she was ashamed of her humble origins
and desired to create a past for herself more in keeping with an ideal image than with the facts. As Joan
Givner says in the introduction to her collection of
Porter's *Conversations*, she invented a

> Catholic upbringing and convent education,
> and . . . an elopement at the age of sixteen from
> a New Orleans convent to marry a man much
> older than herself. . . . She suppresses her age,
> baptismal name, lowly origin as the daughter
> of a poor dirt-farmer, childhood religion, and at
> least one of her husbands." (viii)

"I have no hidden marriages," she once said. "They just escape my mind" (*Conversations* 108).

By way of overview, it may be said that Porter valued (some would say *over-valued*) the strong, dominant, feminine personality, and that she despised the ineffectual, indecisive, and malingering male. The marriages she describes in her fiction are usually unhappy unions, certainly so for the female partners who see themselves stymied by social restrictions that prevent their freedom of action. She distrusted emotionalism and took all possible steps to avoid sentimentality, seeing excessive emotional involvement in the suffering of others as usually not helpful and often downright harmful. She admired action, and she was exasperated with those who (like her Texas father) passively suffered torment without in the least struggling against its causes. There was a strong Calvinist component in her thinking. She really did not believe that people changed or grew or became benign; her treatment of human nature is essentially static. (One might point out that the opposite view—that human beings grow, develop, become "better" as the years pass—is no more "proven" than the opinion that people pretty much remain what they are at about age three or four.) Her failure to write a truly competent full-length novel has been explained by some as her inability to depict change, development, growth;

such a view assumes that such is the nature of the universe. Porter succeeded in the short story form perhaps because that form rarely needs to describe change, growth, development; the realistic short stories that Porter wrote are slices of life as it *is* at a given moment in time.

Porter's sense of dread when she contemplated the devastating poverty of her early childhood was noted by many of her friends. Joan Givner points to a passage from *Ship of Fools* (1962) to show how Porter treated this subject through the memories of Frau Rittersdorf who, while she is wandering on the island of Tenerife, is suddenly ambushed by scenes of youthful poverty:

> Frau Rittersdorf gathered up her things and walked away in a chill of horror as if a bony hand reached out of the past clutching her coldly and drawing her again into the awful wallow of ignorance and poverty and brutish living that she had escaped oh barely—barely! The dirt-floored hut of her grandparents, with the pigpens and the cattle stalls and the chicken roosts all opening into the one room where the whole family lived: the dull mean village cottage of her shoemaking father and her seamstress mother, who felt they had risen high in their world; their ambition for her to

> become a teacher in the village school—Oh, oh,
> oh, cried the whole frightful memory, not only
> in the voices and faces of those dead and gone
> people she had tried all these years to forget, to
> deny; but the very animals, the smothering
> walls and the dirt floors and the stinking shoe
> leather, the taste of lard on the slice of sour
> bread she took to school with her—the very
> bread itself, all rose again out of the deep pit in
> which she had buried them, and one was as
> alive as the other; in a terrible voiceless clamor
> they cried and lamented and accused her,
> soundless as screams in a nightmare. (*Ship of
> Fools* 384)

So dreadful were such memories to Katherine Anne
Porter that she could deal with them only in fiction;
in her own life, denial was her only alternative. The
brilliant descriptions of characters living in poverty
in such works as "He," "The Leaning Tower," and
"Noon Wine" owe a great deal to Porter's dread of
returning to the conditions of her upbringing.

Caricature is a term often used to describe Porter's depiction of human beings. It is a term from
which she did not shrink. Like Dickens, she was
disgusted with those who thought that caricature
was "easy"; the difficult art of focusing in on dominant traits, pervasive mannerisms, compulsive be-

havior patterns, and overriding mindsets was a
worthwhile study, in her view, for the creative artist. Her love affair, during the 1920s, with the great
Mexican caricaturist, Miguel Covarrubias, is perhaps instructive in this regard. Her fiction is, in a
sense, a strategic simplification of moral warfare.
Givner has observed that the theme of Porter's stories as well of her full-length novel is "the arrangement of characters in the triangle of villain, victim,
and not-so-innocent hero/heroine" (*KAP* 193).

An interesting and important facet of Katherine
Anne Porter's life is the large number of influential
literary figures who appreciated and promoted her
work, and were influenced by her creative genius.
The critic Allen Tate, with whom she had a brief
sexual affair (Givner *KAP* 304), Caroline Gordon,
Robert Penn Warren, Malcolm Cowley, Hart Crane,
Glenway Wescott (whose interest in midwestern
regionalism strongly influenced her), Flannery
O'Connor, Carson McCullers, John Peale Bishop,
Kay Boyle, Truman Capote—all these and many,
many more, admired her work, studied it critically,
wrote about her work, and did their best to promote
it in any way they could.

Katherine Anne Porter lived a long and productive life. Although she published relatively little
(when one considers the length of her life), what she

did publish was (except perhaps for *Ship of Fools*) of uniformly high quality. Ironically, as Joan Givner has repeatedly shown, the actual facts of Porter's life cause us to appreciate her achievements more than do the romantic inventions she created to mislead her readers.

3

STORIES OF TEXAS, THE SOUTH, AND SOUTHWEST

Don Graham, in his *Texas: A Literary Portrait* (1985) says that "No one ever wrote better of Texas's Southern past than Katherine Anne Porter, but . . . Porter made up most of it; she invented a gracious Southern world that in fact was much different from the hardscrabble existence of her early upbringing" (63–64). There can be no quarrel with this assertion. But perhaps we are now in a better position to talk about Katherine Anne Porter's motives for presenting the Texas South, not as she knew it to be, but as she consciously created or invented it for literary purposes. And one of those purposes, it can be argued, was to create a mythical Texas past that could ultimately be rejected as unfitting for Miranda Gay, Porter's alter ego in the Miranda stories. Etymologically, "Miranda" is both "one who sees" and "strange and wonderful." The strange, wonderful, and fanciful characteristics of Miranda Gay are transferences from Katherine Anne Porter who summed up all these qualities in her own being.

The Old Order (1944)

Seven of Katherine Anne Porter's stories, collected under the general title, *The Old Order*, are included in *The Leaning Tower and Other Stories* (1944) as well as in *The Collected Stories* (1965). The reader should note that the piece titled "The Old Order" in *The Leaning Tower and Other Stories* was later re-titled "The Journey" in *The Collected Stories*. To speak more correctly, though, four of these pieces ("The Source," "The Journey," "The Witness," and "The Last Leaf") are "sketches"; while the remaining three works ("The Circus," "The Fig Tree," and "The Grave") are more properly referred to as "short stories" in all of which Miranda may be said to learn some sort of lesson (Emmons 5). All seven of these fictional pieces have Texas settings and are quite revealing of Porter's attitudes toward her native state. Unifying the seven pieces is the character of the Texas Grandmother who dominates them all, or—to be more accurate—Miranda Gay's reaction to the Grandmother and those qualities symbolized by the Grandmother and the culture she represents. All these works take place in the Grandmother's household or surrounding farm, and all have to do with the "Southern" past, the myth that must somehow be dealt with by Miranda, the central character from whose point of view the entire group is narrated. The Grandmother, it goes without saying, is a fictional caricature of Porter's Grandmother Porter (Aunt Cat) who managed to weather all difficulties in spite of the incompetent and passive males surrounding her.

If we keep in mind that all seven of these pieces are "Miranda" stories, and that all these stories are to be taken as thematically preliminary to "Old Mortality" (the author's ultimate solution for Miranda, her quest for a "new order"), Porter's intention in grouping them under the general title *The Old Order* seems clear. Miranda will come to demand a *new* order, one that does not require her enslavement to the *old* order, that is the Southern myth, caricatured throughout the seven pieces. This group has no doubt been continuously misread because readers are not on the alert for Porter's keen sense of caricature, though caricature abounds throughout. The most serious misreading of these seven pieces is the one that causes the critic to maintain that Katherine Anne Porter is the champion of a "Gone with the Wind" type of Southern myth. A genuinely close reading, such as Porter had a right to expect during the heydey of the New Criticism, reveals that Porter viciously caricatures Southern manners, Southern character, Southern narratives, the whole Southern mystique with a view to its ultimate rejection. And it is absolutely clear that Miranda in the end *will* reject the Southern myth, though not without a struggle. One effect of such a close reading will be to place Katherine Anne Porter in a more correct situation in regard to Texas literature; if we can come to see her as rejecting the Southern myth (rather than as championing it), we will be in a better position to understand the "Southwestern" and "Texan" qualities of her work. Above all else, the reader must be careful not to miss the subtle humor in the narrative voice of these pieces, humor never being very far away in all of Katherine Anne Porter's work. In addition, the seven pieces in this group must be read as a unit rather than as seven separate and distinct works; otherwise Porter's intentional grouping of the pieces is violated.

Edwin W. Gaston, Jr. has shown that Katherine Anne Porter presents a two-sided view in her *Old Order* stories, both a positive and a negative perspective. On the positive side, Porter, like Faulkner, celebrates the Southern tradition (whether "actual" or contrived through the accretions of historical tradition) that valued courage, honor, hope, pride, compassion, pity, and sacrifice. But on the "pejorative" side, according to Gaston, Porter questions the dominance of the white knights and the virginity of their women; and she suggests that slavery had a darker side than the color of a man's skin (81–82). Ultimately, Porter does not celebrate the Southern myth; she questions its value.

The physical setting of *The Old Order* pieces is not really recognizable as having much to do with Texas, certainly not with the Texas of Katherine Anne Porter's actual upbringing—not that this ought to matter, except to dyed-in-the-wool realists. But the truth needs to be stated at this point. Joan Givner observes that early students of Porter's work, assuming that her life and her literary work were coterminous, had a difficult time when they actually attempted to locate the scenes of her early life:

> When she spoke of herself as a member of the guilt-ridden white pillar crowd, they wondered if the white pillars, more common in the eastern states of the South than in Texas, were those of Austin, San Marcos, and San Antonio. They were not. When Porter described the stately homes of her childhood in fiction and in autobiography, she transferred to the small town of the blackland farming country the ample homes she knew during a five-month period [in 1929] of retreat on the islands of Bermuda. The Porters' small house in Kyle was replaced in her accounts by Hilgrove, the ancestral

home of the Hollis family of Bailey's Bay. The
Porters' shack in the country between Buda
and Mountain City was replaced by the Hol-
lises' house, Cedar Grove. ("Katherine Anne
Porter and the Southwest" 560)

"The Source" (1941)

"The Source" describes the fountainhead of Miranda's strength, the "source" of her strength and
endurance. That source is the Grandmother, a powerful caricature of a towering figure much like Aunt
Cat Porter.

The Grandmother has been called "a metaphor for
Texas" in the stories of Katherine Anne Porter. Perhaps it is more accurate to say that the Grandmother is a metaphor for the Southern myth, a myth
that is highly attractive and even to some extent
valuable, but a myth that, the reader must constantly remember, will ultimately be rejected by Miranda at the conclusion of "Old Mortality." That she
represents both what is admirable and what is re-
pugnant in the Texas and Southern experience
seems quite clear. The Grandmother's admirable
qualities are clearly her independent spirit, self-re-
liance, get-up-and-go, sheer energy, indomitable
will, unshakable faith in her own efforts—all qualities associated with pioneer Texas values. On the

other hand, the Grandmother possesses certain qualities that are threatening to those around her— a domineering personality, intolerance for those who dare to disagree with her, a tendency to run roughshod over the timid and passive, a lack of concern for the projects of others, and a cruel impatience with the slow and sluggish—also qualities associated with the Texas pioneer spirit.

The Grandmother, a widow, otherwise known as "Miss Sophia Jane Rhea," conceives an uncontrollable urge every summer to visit "the farm." Her son, Harry (modeled on Harrison Porter, Katherine Anne Porter's ineffectual father), feigns annoyance, but dares not interfere with any of her schemes. Aunt Nannie is left in charge of the town house, and the Grandmother sets out for her ritualized visit to the farm. Described as "a tireless, just and efficient slave driver of every creature on the place," the Grandmother imposes order, sanitation, and sense on what otherwise would be chaos, filth, and foolishness. Tyrannical and feared though she is, she nevertheless is beloved, a fixed rock in a shifting world. Like her favorite old horse, Fiddler, she knows the duties of her station in life.

After an appropriate number of days, the Grandmother feels compelled to return to the house in town, which "no doubt had gone somewhat astray in her absence."

Worthy of notice are the Negroes—Uncle Jim-billy, Aunt Nannie, Hinry, Littie, Dicey, Bumper, Keg, and Boosker—all given about the same amount of individuality as the horse Fiddler. All is stereo-type and caricature here. The overseer, Mr. Miller, is of course red-headed and given to cruel parsimony in his treatment of the Negroes. All description is subordinated to the character sketch of the Grand-mother, "source" of all that Miranda will ultimately become through acceptance as well as rejection.

"The Journey" (1936)

"The Journey" was titled "The Old Order" in *The Leaning Tower and Other Stories*, and it is unfortu-nate that this title was changed, for it is really the central nervous system of the seven pieces now sub-ordinated under the general title *The Old Order*. "The Journey" in fact ambiguously describes "order" according to the *old*, that is old Nannie and the old Grandmother, both now nearing death, having com-pleted their arduous "journey" together throughout a long lifetime, as well as "the old order," that is, the rigid dogmas (thoroughly caricatured) held to in times gone by concerning how life ought to be lived, especially female life and the life generally recom-mended for children.

The sketch deals with the relationship between

the Grandmother and an ex-slave, Old Nannie, that relationship symbolizing Southern manners in "the old order." The two old women love to work together on their quilting, and it is their joint effort to "piece together" a picture of the past, each making an individual and eccentric contribution; the Grandmother has a fine memory for dates, but she cannot attach the proper significance to the dates; old Nannie can recall names and trivial circumstances surrounding important events, but she has no interest in dates. But together they quilt a pattern of the past. So long have the two been companions that in some ways they have become indistinguishable. As Winfred Emmons observes, "the pronoun 'they' dominates almost a third of the piece" (13). The reader is not quite sure whether old Nannie is an extension of the Grandmother or whether the Grandmother is an extension of old Nannie; the point is that black and white have lived together so long that the untying of the knot is no longer really possible.

The interdependence of the two women, one black and one white, is best illustrated by the fact that the Grandmother nurses a black child of Nannie's during a period of Nannie's sickness; the Grandmother's independence and essential kindness are nowhere better illustrated than in this action. And no other element in *The Old Order* stories questions so boldly the Southern myth that Porter is in the act of bringing down.

The atmosphere is stereotypically comic throughout. The Negroes, we are told, "loved lying under the hackberry grove back of the barns playing seven-up, and eating watermelons." The two old women chat endlessly about their children, their sewing, their disappointments in life. Always they talk of the past, only the past. And it is the family past that is most compelling. Here we are given in fictionalized and distorted form Katherine Anne Porter's family history. The Grandmother's reminiscences of her dead husband recall the ineffectual male, derived from Katherine Anne Porter's attitude toward her own Texas father: "lack of aim, failure to act at crises, a philosophic detachment from practical affairs, a tendency to set projects on foot and then leave them to perish or to be finished by someone else; and a profound conviction that everyone around him should be happy to wait upon him hand and foot." Some readers will no doubt consider the preceding quotation an attack on masculinity in general. Nevertheless, Granny is, and has always been, a woman unable to avoid continual enslavement by males. No matter how independent of spirit she becomes, that fact remains. "She could not help it, she despised men. She despised them and was ruled by them."

Shiftless men, husband and sons, have little trouble overcoming her better sense and scruples. All she really has left is a stern religious view of "duty" that—despite her own doubts which she is careful to keep to herself—she attempts to impose on all those around her.

The scrupulous reader will observe the attack upon the outmoded Southern ideology, especially as it affects the role of women. This sketch merely reinforces the strong feminist bias of the entire group. The two old women, one white and one black, are in agreement concerning the Southern myth: women got a raw deal. Texas, somebody once said, was hell on women and horses. Certainly Southern ideology, including that of Porter's Texas, was *hell* on women.

"The Witness" (1944)

"The Witness" (1944) is a character sketch of Uncle Jimbilly, handyman and former slave, an individual not allowed to live his life truly, but only as a "witness" to the greatest of American moral blights, Negro slavery. Here caricature reaches a sublime height. Uncle Jimbilly is an ostensible "Uncle Tom" figure who masks his suffering in a ritualized shuffle of conversation with the three young children for whom he whittles tombstones to be used for various dead animals. Wielding his bowie knife with skill, and his storytelling gift with gusto, he is an artist-figure preoccupied with death, essentially death of the spirit, the legacy of slavery. Only a very dense reader of this sketch could believe that Katherine Anne Porter portrays this ex-slave as happy or contented. And Uncle Jimbilly's description of slave torture, possibly exaggerated but effective nonetheless, informs us of Porter's knowledge that slavery was upheld by physical power, not moral ideology. Uncle Jimbilly is an educator in the Uncle Remus tradition, but his mournful tone when speaking of the old days under slavery makes him something more than this. Uncle Jimbilly's refusal to carve "Safe in Heaven" on a little wooden tombstone for a jackrabbit underscores his private rejection of Southern platitudes, a rejection that is Katherine Anne Porter's also.

"The Circus" (1935)

"The Circus" is a fictionalized treatment of childhood fear of death. Miranda is introduced to death in an unexpected way and is unprepared to deal with the subject. Death, like sex (represented by the nasty boys, under the circus bleachers, trying to look up the women's skirts), is as yet unfathomable to Miranda.

The Calvinistic Grandmother, who thoroughly

disapproves of circuses, nevertheless permits the
child Miranda go to the circus only because of the
family reunion. A surfeit of sensations passes over
Miranda, who is unprepared for such excitement.
"An enormous brass band seemed to explode right
at Miranda's ear. She jumped, quivered, thrilled
blindly and almost forgot to breathe as sound and
color and smell rushed together and poured through
her skin and hair and beat in her head and hands
and feet and pit of her stomach." Then the image of
Death:

> A creature in a blousy white overall with
> ruffles at the neck and ankles, with bone-white
> skull and chalk-white face, with tufted eye-
> brows far apart in the middle of his forehead,
> the lids in a black sharp angle, a long scarlet
> mouth stretching back into sunken cheeks,
> turned up at the corners in a perpetual bitter
> grimace of pain, astonishment, not smiling,
> pranced along a wire stretched down the center
> of the ring, balancing a long thin pole with
> little wheels at either end. (*Collected Stories*
> 344)

Miranda becomes hysterical, comprehending the
threat of death but unable to articulate the genuine
horror she feels. She covers her eyes and screams,
and her father orders Dicey, the black hired girl, to

take Miranda home—in considerable disgrace, it turns out, for she has missed a great deal of fun. Later that night, amid visions of the malignant dwarf who had taunted her at the circus, Miranda cries out in her dreams and has to be comforted by Dicey. Miranda learns that she has a great need of companionship. Significantly, she fears the darkness: "if only Dicey might not turn out the lights and leave her to the fathomless terrors of the darkness where sleep could overtake her once more." Darkness and sleep have become for her at this point death and dissolution. The threatened fall of a circus clown, accompanied by a "fall" into knowledge of the real world, makes this in one sense a story of "the fortunate fall." The Freudian doctrine that dreams of falling indicate fear of death is at work in this story. The Texas Grandmother's fundamentalist, essentially Calvinistic notions of fallen human nature and conduct make such an interpretation of this story tenable.

"The Last Leaf" (1944)

"The Last Leaf" is a comic character sketch, in high caricature, of old Nannie. But caricature or not, the essential nobility of old Nannie and, by extension, of blacks under slavery and segregation, comes through. In her old age, looking forward to death, she demonstrates her independent spirit. As the amusingly detached narrator says, she "was no more the faithful old servant Nannie, a freed slave: she was an aged Bantu woman of independent means, sitting on the steps breathing the free air." She even takes up smoking—on a corncob pipe. Permitted by Mr. Harry to live in a vacant old cabin, she at last has a chance to live her own life. The whites are quite surprised to see her contentment; it had always seemed to them that old Nannie was happy among her white employers.

Milking the comic side of this story (which probably owes a great deal to Faulkner's comic stories of the South), the narrator informs us that Uncle Jimbilly and old Nannie were once husband and wife. But theirs was a marriage of convenience, arranged by white masters; no reason exists for the marriage to continue. Nannie rejects Uncle Jimbilly's timid and tentative bid to come to live with her. She will not spend her last days waiting on a man.

Old Nannie is comically triumphant over males, both white and black, in this sketch; a distinctively feminist ideology lurks just beneath the surface of the ironic narrative. Indeed, "the old order" as Porter imaginatively depicts it was, when we allow for the overstated caricature, a benevolent matriarchy, contrasting with the *actual* old order that was hell on women and horses.

"The Fig Tree" (1960)

"The Fig Tree" was actually completed in Bermuda in 1929, but the story was not published until June of 1960 when it appeared in *Harper's Magazine*. Porter referred to it as "the last of the Miranda stories" (Hendrick 47). The story's title suggests an affinity for St. Augustine's *Confessions*, and the story does deal with a guilty conscience, or at least a consciousness of guilt. Miranda buries a dead chicken under a fig tree, only to fancy that she hears it uttering the faint syllables "Weep, Weep." Later, on a visit with the family to great Aunt Eliza's farm, she is told that a similar "Weep, Weep" sound comes from the tree-frogs. Miranda is thus consoled, for perhaps she did not, after all, bury a live chick underneath the fig tree in town.

But the real subject of "The Fig Tree" is suffocation, symbolized by the "Weep, Weep" sound of the supposedly suffocating chick buried beneath the fig tree. Suffocation is brought about by the culture of the old order, the treatment of children, the keeping of knowledge from the young (just as their skin must be protected from freckles by exposure to the sun).

Children are therefore the helpless victims of the old order, unable to breathe freely in any sense. The relationship of this story to Blake's "The Chimney Sweeper" has often been pointed out, with good reason.

Miranda learns that her Grandmother and her Great Aunt Eliza bicker like the sisters they are, that they are not in agreement on very many topics (Eliza's dipping snuff, for example), and that nothing is very certain. Great Aunt Eliza's scientific interests make for an objective backdrop for this story. Nobody knows for sure about the wonders seen in her telescope; and nobody knows for sure about the received truths of the old order. For Miranda, certainty now comes into question. Katherine Anne Porter, certainly, is questioning received truths that she herself had learned from the old order.

"The Grave" (1935)

"The Grave" (1935) so effectively displays its symbolic structure that some critics have referred to this work as "contrived," forgetting that all stories are contrived. Like "The Fig Tree," this story deals with death, but this time the terror of death is intermixed with the fear and wonder associated with sexuality. The setting is 1903 on the Texas farm owned by the

Grandmother. After the Grandmother's death, some of the land has to be sold off for the benefit of the surviving children. It so happens that the family cemetery lies on the part of the land that is to be sold, necessitating the removal of the bodies for re-burial in the new cemetery in town. Death, hovering always near, pervades this marvelous tale. The un-articulated wonder felt by the two children, Miranda (aged nine) and Paul (aged twelve), constitutes the mournful tone.

The two children examine the open, empty graves. Miranda finds a silver dove, Paul a gold ring; appro-priately, they exchange treasures. The silver dove had been the screw-head for a coffin, the gold ring once a wedding ring. The poetic associations of the dove and the ring resound throughout the remain-der of the story.

Of some interest in this story is Miranda's social sense. In spite of her dislike of and disagreement with established norms of female dress, she never-theless suffers from the scornful attitude of those that she considers her inferiors. The reader gains some understanding here of Katherine Anne Por-ter's preoccupation with clothes and jewels; and, alongside this preoccupation, one senses the ironic narrator's contempt for the whole subject. Ambiva-lence, as ever, reigns in Porter's fiction. The disgust,

yet shame, that Miranda feels about hand-me-down
clothes is superbly presented in the caricature of the
ignorant old Texas ladies:

> They slanted their gummy old eyes side-
> ways at the granddaughter and said, "Ain't you
> ashamed of yoself, Missy? It's against the
> Scriptures to dress like that. Whut yo Pappy
> thinkin about?" Miranda, with her powerful so-
> cial sense, which was like a fine set of antennae
> radiating from every pore of her skin, would
> feel ashamed because she knew well it was
> rude and ill-bred to shock anybody, even bad-
> tempered old crones, though she had faith in
> her father's judgment. . . . (*Collected Stories*
> 365)

Miranda is a tom-boy and is beginning to become
conscious of the fact that such an androgynous existence (we are rather pointedly told that she did not
care for dolls) is considered inappropriate, perhaps
even anti-Scriptural.

When Paul shoots a rabbit and skins it, it is dis-
covered that the female rabbit had been pregnant
with young. The horror and wonder of this sight is
taken in, the two children understanding the connection between human and animal life. The unborn
infant rabbits are described in essentially human
terms:

> . . . there they were, dark gray, their sleek
> wet down lying in minute, even ripples, like a
> baby's head just washed, their unbelievably
> small delicate ears folded close, their little
> blind faces almost featureless.

Looking upon this sight, Miranda intuits the knowledge of sexuality. Miranda, feeling pity and horror, refuses to take the fur for her dolls. And she promises Paul never to tell anyone about the sight she has seen.

Some twenty years later, Miranda, in a strange city (clearly Mexican), comes upon a sight that brings back to her the experience that she had so long ago buried in her consciousness:

> An Indian vendor had held up before her a
> tray of dyed sugar sweets, in the shapes of all
> kinds of small creatures: birds, baby chicks,
> baby rabbits, lambs, baby pigs. They were in
> gay colors and smelled of vanilla, maybe. . . . It
> was a very hot day and the smell in the market,
> with its piles of raw flesh and wilting flowers,
> was like the mingled sweetness and corruption
> she had smelled that other day in the empty
> cemetery at home.

Suddenly, the buried memory returns to her. The human memory is thus a womb, harboring undeveloped and obscure images that will emerge when the need arises. Birth, death, and sexuality merge in Miranda's consciousness.

"The Grave," with its treatment of materials buried in the creative mind, reveals the effect of Katherine Anne Porter's Texas childhood upon her subsequent literary career; the Texas childhood was always there, if only a means could be found to put it to use. As Emmons points out, "The Grave" develops the sense of place more thoroughly than do any of the other "Old Order" sketches (23).

Another important point to be made about "The Grave" is that in this story Katherine Anne Porter establishes a creative connection between Texas and Mexico, showing the reader that the girl was mother of the woman; the sense of place could be carried over from childhood to maturity.

"Old Mortality" (1938)

"Old Mortality" is partly set, like the stories included in *The Old Order*, in the Texas Grandmother's household, where the aroma of nostalgia is blended with the odor of death. The story is somewhat reminiscent of James Joyce's "The Dead" (1914) and perhaps of Faulkner's "A Rose for Emily" (1930), with an ending that distinctly evokes the conclusion of Joyce's *Portrait of the Artist as a Young Man* (1916); indeed, one would be justified in subtitling this story: "Portrait of the Artist as a Young Woman." The dead exercise considerable power over the living; the legends of the past threaten to overpower the reality of the present; the present is stifled by the odorous past. Miranda, nevertheless, will make her break with the powerful past and launch out on her own journey, an odyssey of self-discovery.

"Old Mortality" is arranged into three parts. "Part I: 1885–1902" describes the legend of Miranda's Aunt Amy and Uncle Gabriel, handed down in the family over a period of many years. As a child, Miranda has heard her relatives speak continually with reverential nostalgia of her now-dead Aunt Amy ("beloved" in Latin) who had been known for her grace and beauty. It seems that no woman living in the present has any hope of measuring up to Aunt Amy's beauty and grace. Only gradually does Miranda come to realize that these accounts of her aunt bear little resemblance to the facts. Romantic nostalgia and all the trappings of folk romance pervade these musty tales. Of foremost importance, from Miranda's point of view, will be her own difficulty in measuring up, ever, to the standards of grace and beauty set so long ago by Amy, the beloved. Romance is the real subject, the intoxicating and addictive aura cast by the past upon the present, leading to enervation in the present day. Only gradually does Miranda come to doubt the greatness and beauty of Amy and of the romantic tradition that she symbolizes.

The tale of Amy's unfortunate death, and the grief of Gabriel, have been inscribed permanently in Miranda's imagination. But as Miranda matures, she comes to desire a more realistic view of the old order that Aunt Amy so vividly represents to her.

"Part II: 1904" is set in New Orleans where Miranda and her older sister Maria are "immured" in a Catholic school, the Convent of the Child Jesus. It is in this section that Miranda actually meets Uncle Gabriel and learns that he is an alcoholic gambler, an ineffectual yearner after sudden and unearned profits, and a disappointed lover. Married now to Miss Honey, he strains under a heavy yoke of responsibility. In short, he is a bum. The contrast between what Miranda had been told about Gabriel and the actual man is indeed shocking. Miranda will learn in the future not to take tales of the past with such seriousness. This is simply one more step that Miranda must take to shake off "the old order."

"Part III: 1912" details Miranda's journey back to Texas for Uncle Gabriel's funeral. Gabriel, having drunk himself to death because of his inconsolable grief over Amy (reminiscent, as usual, of Harrison Porter's lifelong grief over his dead wife), has been brought home to be buried next to her. There seems to be no surprise in the fact that Uncle Gabriel had no desire to be buried next to his second wife, Miss Honey, who had expired earlier. Gabriel lived only for his lost Amy and for his racing horses. On the train Miranda meets Cousin Eva Parrington, a magnificent caricature of the feminist agitator.

Here we get a completely different picture of Amy and the culture of the old order that she represents. Her aunt Amy was actually a spoiled, selfish, sex-driven female who unthinkingly sacrificed others to her petty whims. Porter here ruthlessly undermines the absurd Southern myth of the virginity of the white female. Jane DeMouy observes that "'Old Mortality' is the story of Miranda's confrontation with the most formidable archetype her society can offer: the Southern belle, a nineteenth-century American manifestation of the virgin love goddess" (147). As might be expected, Miranda, learning from Cousin Eva Parrington and others, finds the myth of virginity an empty one. Furthermore, we see that a life dedicated to a cause, as Eva Parrington's is, can end in meaninglessness, though in this case meaning is clearly in the eye of the individual reader/beholder. Since Eva Parrington is the champion of women's rights, it is only fit that Miranda be exposed to her at this juncture.

At the conclusion of "Old Mortality," Miranda is ready to strike out on her own, unencumbered by the romantic view of the past:

Her mind closed stubbornly against remembering, not the past but the legend of the past,
other people's memory of the past, at which she
had spent her life peering in wonder like a
child at a magic-lantern show. Ah, but there is
my own life to come yet, she thought, my own
life now and beyond. I don't want any promises,
I won't have false hopes, I won't be romantic
about myself. I can't live in their world any
longer, she told herself, listening to the voices
back of her. Let them tell their stories to each
other. Let them go on explaining how things
happened. I don't care. At least I can know the
truth about what happens to me, she assured
herself silently, making a promise to herself, in
her hopefulness, her ignorance. (*Collected Stories* 221)

Miranda is guilty of "ignorant" thinking in this case
only in the sense that all events in life are subject to
interpretation, even those events that happen to
oneself; and, in time, Miranda—like all the rest of
us—will come to understand that her own interpretation of her own life is not necessarily the best or
the most current interpretation; nevertheless, it is
the interpretation by which she must live.

Those who have seen "Old Mortality" as fiction in
the "Gone with the Wind" tradition miss the point
being made by this narrative. Porter's message is
that we ought not be bound by romantic and illu-

sionary notions of the past, but rather pursue our own journey in our own way, gropingly if necessary. The necessity of shedding the dead past is intensified by Porter's making of that dead past a rather absurd stereotype of the "Southern" ideal of womanhood and manhood. Aunt Amy is not, it is clear, a worthy heroine for Miranda's emulation; and Uncle Gabriel Breaux must be dismissed as a true hero in any sense. Far from romanticizing the Old South, this story, through pitiless caricature, rejects the very basis of the Southern myth.

Whatever the truth about Aunt Amy and Uncle Gabriel, Miranda at the end of "Old Mortality" is determined to live her own life in her own way. Miranda, grown to young womanhood, will also be the heroine of "Pale Horse, Pale Rider," and will continue her farewell to the past as she pursues her career in journalism and literature.

In another connection, the story has turned—in one of its many facets—into a feminist ideological tract. Porter is quite careful to hide her own feelings about Miranda's Aunt Eva, the homely spinster and Latin teacher who was dismissed from her teaching position because of her feminist agitation. But Eva is the new Eve (or is she the "evening" of the past and present?), promising new opportunities for the modern woman of the type that Miranda is in the process of becoming. Aunt Eva's cynicism is not altogether unlike that of her creator; and her utter realism is an antidote to Miranda's romantic tendencies. Clearly, Miranda and Aunt Eva, not to mention Katherine Anne Porter, are sisters under the skin.

In every possible way, Porter reinforces the view that the dead past ought not enslave the living present. Gabriel may wail over the grave of his beloved Amy, but he cannot summon her from the dead. He blows his horn uselessly. The most that can be hoped for him is that he will be buried, along with his outdated romantic notions, quickly and decently beside his beloved Amy. He is a caricature of the wasted life.

"Pale Horse, Pale Rider" (1938)

"Pale Horse, Pale Rider," another narrative in the "Miranda" series, is set in Denver during the 1918 influenza epidemic after the First World War. It has as one of its central characters Adam Barclay, a Texas-born officer. The story takes place six years after Uncle Gabriel's funeral (referred to in the conclusion of "Old Mortality"), and is therefore important in the depiction of Miranda's continuing development. Having shucked off "the old order," Miranda now is engaged in the world of professional writing. The rather spare plot suggests, as is usual in Porter's fiction, a great deal more than it actually states. Essentially, it is the narrative of a fleeting love affair between Miranda, now a young Southern newspaperwoman (such as Porter herself was during her days in Denver) and a vaguely realized young Texas-born soldier, Adam Barclay. It is worthy of note that Adam Barclay is the only lover of Miranda ever portrayed by Katherine Anne Porter (DeMouy 163).

Informing this story is a conflation of the Judaeo-Christian myth of the Garden (before the Fall) and the Greek myth of Aphrodite and Adonis (DeMouy 163–664). The Adam/Eve/Miranda motif is clear, but the Aphrodite/Adonis/Adam Barclay/Miranda theme must be gleaned from the poetically evocative passages of description—passages whose beauty is unsurpassed anywhere in English or American fiction.

Aphrodite, goddess of love, conceived a passion for the beautiful youth, Adonis (associated in some Greek legends with the Sun). But Aphrodite's husband was Ares, god of war. Ares caused Adonis to be slain by a wild boar. Where Adonis's blood spilled there sprang up anemones (symbols of resurrection). DeMouy cites Porter's description of Adam Barclay as evidence of her concern with the solar myth:

> . . . his innocence and nobility of purpose
> mark him as a prelapsarian Adam. But just as
> he is Adam, he is also Adonis. In shades of gold,
> tan, brown, and green—"hay colored"—he sug-
> gests simultaneously growing vegetation and
> the harvest time in which the story is set. True
> to the connotations of the name Adonis, Adam
> is more comely than any other man, dressed in
> his well-tailored uniform with the "manly
> smell of scentless soap, freshly cleaned leather
> and freshly washed skin" about him. Miranda
> repeatedly admires his good looks, his "ex-
> traordinary face, smooth and fine and
> golden. . . . More than anything else, however,
> he reflects Adonis as a sacrifice. (163–64)

And as "the lank greenish stranger" from Miranda's
dream, Adam—in his olive drab uniform—unites
the Adam and Adonis motifs of the story. And it is
Adam's birth, death, and symbolic resurrection that
promise new life in place of the old. Adam Barclay's
Texas origin shows us what Texas meant to Katherine Anne Porter.

From this perspective, it is somewhat easier to
understand Katherine Anne Porter's outrage at being told that "Pale Horse, Pale Rider" did not contain "indigenous" Texas subject matter.

For Porter personally, the story is an allegorical
depiction of her troubled relationship to Texas. To

deny the Texas connection of this narrative is, in this restricted sense, to miss a part of Porter's intention. The name Adam Barclay suggests, of course, some sort of rebirth or resurrection. And it is exactly this that Katherine Anne Porter seems to be writing about in this powerful story. So much of the story is taken up with Miranda under sedation, in a surreal world halfway between life and death, that the reader senses somehow that death and rebirth are pertinent thematic concerns. The five dreams that Miranda experiences become part of the structural complexity of the tale.

Miranda's life as a journalist in Denver is doubtless closely related to Katherine Anne Porter's actual experiences. And the "local color" involved in the descriptions of the city will interest many readers. The war-time mentality, Porter's chauvinistic patriotism, and the aura of dream makes this one of her most intriguing stream-of-consciousness tales. Only "The Jilting of Granny Weatherall" rivals it in that respect. But our interest in this discourse in chiefly the Texas connection of Katherine Anne Porter's fiction.

Adam Barclay, Texas born but now removed from the primeval Eden, functions as a metaphor for Porter's nostalgic memories of her home state. As ideal Adamic hero, Barclay, molded from the original Texas soil, must serve his purpose and quietly de-

part. The fact that he must be sacrificed (though
never forgotten) is indicative of Porter's courage and
determination at this point in her career. Adam dies
in the influenza epidemic, and so does a part of Miranda's world. Adam (called "the lamb" on one occasion) will be offered up as appeasement to the god of
war, or as innocence to the god of cynicism, or as the
memory of Texas to a great writer in the act of tran-
scending her childhood experiences. Adam Barclay
is in one sense Miranda's (and Katherine Anne Porter's) "double." With Adam Barclay dies a lingering
innocence, gentleness, and passivity that Porter will
now no longer need in her quest for artistic dominance. Porter was in this sense "reborn" during the
1918 influenza epidemic in Denver.

Porter herself, as is well known, came close to
death in Denver during the selfsame influenza epidemic that she describes in "Pale Horse, Pale Rider."
The faint touch of Texas (the Texas-born soldier)
reminds us that her breaking away from her roots
was not to be easy. But the "refugee from Indian
Creek" was never, ultimately, to forsake her homeland.

"The Jilting of Granny Weatherall" (1929)

The wasted life, a frequently recurring theme in
Porter's fiction, is in fact, one of the major themes of

"The Jilting of Granny Weatherall," another of the stories dealing with the Grandmother. Craig Clifford has written that "the open spaces of the West only gave us a false impression that we could plunder and pollute without noticeable consequence." But in addition, the symbolic richness of the open spaces might just as well show the creative writer "nature as a symbol of the inexhaustible meaning of being, rather than the inexhaustible availability of raw materials for so-called human purposes" ("Horseman, Hang on" 50–51). A dominant theme of "The Jilting of Granny Weatherall" (1929) is *waste*, the waste of human as well as natural resources. As the reader will recall, Miranda—in "The Grave"— had imbibed the rigid dogma of the Texas poor: "Wastefulness was vulgar. It was also a sin. These were truths; she heard them repeated many times and never once disputed" (*Collected Stories* 365). More tragic, more sinful than all else was a wasted, or meaningless life. Though natural resources were scarce to Granny Weatherall, meaning proved to be inexhaustible.

"The Jilting of Granny Weatherall" should be read in close connection with *The Old Order* stories, since it is clearly a fictional treatment of the death of the same Grandmother who appears in the earlier stories, despite the difference in names of characters (Gaston 85). The strength of her character is made manifest in the contrasting weaknesses of her children. The matriarchy that she represents will begin to pass away with her death.

Wayne Booth has praised Porter's willingness to forego realistic dialogue (or monologue) in this story:

> Katherine Anne Porter's "The Jilting of Granny Weatherall" is a masterful "inside" presentation of the last moments of the heroine. By resisting the temptation to be literal and realistic in the heroine's language, and by drawing together in the final thoughts all the threads of the "jilting" theme, she achieves a very moving death. (61–62)

Because the Grandmother confuses, at the last moment, her lover George and the savior, Jesus Christ, neither of whom show up, it is arguable that she is to be "jilted" even in her extremity. Needless to say, nobody knows *precisely* what thoughts go through the mind of a dying person. But Porter's depiction of Granny Weatherall's death certainly is not realistic in the ordinary sense; the presentation is aesthetic, not objective.

Daniel and Madeline Barnes argue, in "The Secret Sin of Granny Weatherall" (1969), that Granny Weatherall was pregnant at the time when George jilted her; the evidence cited is the constant reference to "babies." They maintain that what "is not given back" is her virginity, symbolic of her feminine integrity. If this argument is correct, Granny Weatherall is another portrait of the archetypal "Southern belle"—an incarnation of this mythical creature in a form rather different from Amy in "Old Mortality." Joann Cobb, in an interesting essay, "Pascal's Wager and Two Modern Losers," (the "two modern losers" being Granny Weatherall in Porter's story, and The Misfit in Flannery O'Connor's "A Good Man Is Hard to Find") finds that Granny Weatherall loses out, theologically speaking; in order to avoid the "Hell" of despair, Granny, the argument goes, puts up with a less than satisfactory life *in this world*, hoping for a better world hereafter. The "loss," from this point of view, is the loss of genuine self-fulfillment in the world of the present. But it is difficult for the secular reader to think of Granny Weatherall (or the Misfit either, for that matter) as a loser in any real sense. Granny, after all, does come to love the man who was her second choice; and she is genuinely devoted to her children. Since she cannot have the man she loves, she comes to love the man she has. Despite her preoccupation with one traumatic event in her early life, the day of being jilted at the altar, she has managed, despite all odds, to live a meaningful life. If Granny has suppressed all real hope for human happiness in this world, hoping for a better life in the world to come, then surely she misjudged. The life she *did* live in this world was quite meaningful—if, as usual, we will agree to relativism; meaningful, compared to what? Surely, Granny Weatherall loses a great deal through her preoccupation with one dreadful moment of her past; but she gains a great deal, the honest reader feels, through her ability to do the work that has to be done, whatever her private sufferings. Waste there is, symbolized poignantly by the wedding cake that is thrown out and never eaten, but accomplishment also. Granny has truly, as her name patently suggests, "weathered all" in spite of the adverse conditions of her existence. Her spite is, in fact, the source of her spunk. She is an excellent representative of the Texas spirit, Porter's Grandmother (Aunt Cat) in a superb Texas incarnation. Her life has been lived with gusto, as if she went around only once.

One might well compare Granny Weatherall in Porter's story with Letty in Dorothy Scarborough's *The Wind* (1925) from a regionalist point of view. Despite the fact that Scarborough describes the gradual onset of insanity brought on by the wind, which symbolizes the cruelty of the natural world, her work is not by any means as "psychological" as Porter's. The naturalistic writer like Scarborough does not, it goes without saying, attempt to deal realistically with the stream of consciousness; yet Porter, not at all a naturalist, manages to accomplish both naturalistic truth and "psychological realism." One slight master stroke of the artist can illustrate this truth, the two-sentence description of Granny Weatherall's experience in the Texas landscape: "She had fenced in a hundred acres once, digging the post holes herself and clamping the wires with just a negro boy to help. That changed a woman" (*Collected Stories* 83). The understatement is evident to anyone who has ever worked on fences in Texas.

"He" (1927)

"He," the first story by Porter to deal with "Texas" material, originally appeared in Porter's first story collection, *Flowering Judas and Other Stories* (1930). The power of this story is demonstrated by the numerous critical attitudes toward Mrs. Whipple, mother of the retarded child, referred to only as "He." Bruce W. Jorgensen, in "'He' as Tragedy," (1982) provides an excellent summary of these critical wranglings.

On one level, "He" is—like "Holiday"—a portrayal of the defective child in a hostile environment; on a slightly different level, the story—like *Noon Wine*—depicts the miserable life of poverty-stricken Texas sharecroppers. The typographical necessity of capitalizing the personal pronoun *He* when referring to the character, a profoundly retarded child, is subtly suggestive of legends of the sacred idiot (He blithely leads a frightful bull without harm to himself); on the other hand, the character's lack of a genuine name tends to make him something less than truly human.

At issue are three questions: Do the parents (especially Mrs. Whipple, from whose point of view the narrative develops) really wish their idiot child dead? Do they genuinely love the child? Or do they merely pretend to cherish their offspring in order to garner and maintain social approval? The answer to all these questions is, of course, yes and no; for it is the ambivalence of parental love that is the subject of this powerful story. It is quite possible for parents of a defective child to harbor pity, compassion, and love for the same child which they secretly despise and would like to see dead. Just as it is possible to joke and be serious at the same time, so it is quite conceivable that parents can both love and hate their own child at the same moment. It is especially the mother of the child who commands our sympathy in this story, for it is she who feels affection and pity for small and helpless things that of necessity must be sacrificed to the order of things as they are.

Mrs. Whipple, mother-figure, instinctively responds to small, helpless things, even though she understands—by virtue of extreme poverty—the necessity of sacrifice of those very small and helpless things. Contemplating the scalded pig that has been killed for a visitation of relatives, she muses: "the sight of the pig scraped pink and naked made her sick. It was simply a shame the way things had to happen." Significantly, Mrs. Whipple had already sensed the affinity between her own helpless child and the frightened pig. When He was dispatched to bring her the little pig, which had to be forcibly removed from its mother (a foreshadowing of her own parental fate),

> the little black squirming thing was screeching like a baby in a tantrum, stiffening its back and stretching its mouth to the ears. Mrs. Whipple took the pig with her face stiff and sliced its throat with one stroke. When He saw the blood He gave a great jolting breath and ran away.

The pig, which "screeches like a baby" is thus a displacement for Mrs. Whipple's parental emotions. And her fate is not only to slice the throat of a pig "with her face stiff" (suppressing pity with great difficulty), but—at the end, when she must sacrifice Him for the very survival of the family—"to cry, frightfully" and wrap her arms tightly around him. And the fact that He has been effectively relegated

to a sub-human, or animal, status, actually en-
hances, rather than detracts from, the pity that Mrs.
Whipple feels but cannot fully articulate.

But there can be no doubt that the desire for social
approval is strong among the good country people,
and especially in Mrs. Whipple, treated in this story.
Mrs. Whipple, as her name suggests, is a whip to
her own conscience, but a subtle whip, as her various rationalizations demonstrate. Debra Moddelmog
says that "although she would not admit the fact,
even to herself, Mrs. Whipple's relationship with
Him is dictated by what others would think, not by
motherly love or tenderness" (119). But if this is so,
might it not be in order for us to ask of Moddelmog
if there is *any human emotion whatsoever* that is not
tainted in this manner *in any human being whom-
ever*? Is it not, in short, the ability to harbor essentially conflicting emotions within our breast at any
one time that marks our human condition? The fact
that Mrs. Whipple is constantly concerned with
what others might think does not, in any way, con-
trovert her equal love and concern for her child. As
social animals, we express emotion socially, even
those unconscious emotions that we do not admit,
even to ourselves.

Mrs. Whipple's motive for dehumanizing Him is
clear: this is the only way she can justify the treatment of Him that her circumstances require her to

perform. She *must*, consciously or unconsciously, think of Him as something less than human; otherwise, she would have to confess herself guilty of a desire to destroy her own child. It is, in fact, this desperate strategy itself that reveals Mrs. Whipple's love for her son. We as readers are reminded, ever so subtly, that we each *whip*/kill the thing we love, there being little reason to kill the thing to which we are indifferent. And Mrs. Whipple is *not* indifferent to the fate of her son.

The ironic tone of the story seems designed, as several critics have observed, to counterbalance any possible drift, on the reader's part, in the direction of sentimentality; the neutral, cold-blooded, objective, matter-of-fact narration corrects what could have become simply another tear-jerker.

Jorgensen notes that numerous critics have failed to understand the genuine pathos of this story. Some have condemned Mrs. Whipple for her refusal to face the facts; others have self-righteously accused her of an excessive desire for social approval. Emmons notes sarcastically that Mrs. Whipple "practices the eleventh commandment, which is to put up the appearance of virtue if one cannot manage the real thing" (26). What practically all critics of this story have failed to bring into proper focus is the hard-scrabble existence of sharecropping Texas farmers. This social and economic context, the same, essentially, as that faced by the Thompsons of *Noon Wine*, makes moralistic judgments irrelevant. Jorgensen quotes Myron M. Liberman's sensible statement: "the burden of the story is the terrible question of how many of us could have succeeded in giving love where Mrs. Whipple failed" (109). The answer, surely, is that not many of us could—under the dreadfully circumscribed conditions imposed by the author—measure up so well as Mrs. Whipple under such adversity.

Quite simply put, it is more difficult for the poor and disadvantaged to express love than it is for the privileged. Survival is, after all, a mighty motivation. One might quote at this point what Dreiser said of his heroine, Sister Carrie, who was accused of immoral use of her body to improve her situation in the world: "the voice of want made answer for her."

Emmons summarizes the thematic content of this story well:

> People like the Whipples are deserving of sympathy, but no purpose is served in sentimentalizing them. Inherently they are neither virtuous nor vicious, nor are they any more contemptible than any people are when bereft of civilizing influences. If they are deserving of punishment for their failure to produce order and beauty out of their chaotic lives, the lives they lead are punishment enough. (28)

In other words, the Whipples are people just like us. That is the true horror of this story properly contemplated.

Jorgensen's final evaluation of this story is impressive.

> No one in our century has put the short story to nobler use—or to stricter discipline—than Katherine Anne Porter, and "He," a compact tragedy in the low mimetic mode of realistic fiction, is simply one of the finer instances of that fact: a classic story written "with all the truth and tenderness and severity" that Miss Porter intended as the hallmark of all her work. (115)

One could argue convincingly that "He," Porter's first "Texas" story is Katherine Anne Porter's finest creation. But criticism has not by any means finished with this story.

"The Downward Path to Wisdom" (1939)

"The Downward Path to Wisdom" and "Rope" were excluded by Winfred Emmons, in his *Katherine Anne Porter: The Regional Stories*, from his list of Texas stories; Emmons remarked that these stories "might have been set in Texas but Oregon would have done just as well" (5). The best corrective for

Emmons's opinion might be, one could argue, Larry McMurtry's delightfully naughty essay "Eros in Archer County," included in his *In a Narrow Grave*, in which he describes various sexual taboos dealt with by rural Texans through various Victorian-like strategies. The sexual motifs of both these stories owe a great deal to Katherine Anne Porter's repressive rural Texas girlhood. And the fact that Porter had a Texas setting in mind, at least to some degree, is seen in the pastoral atmosphere and in the dialogue. Besides, the story is probably related to the "Miranda" stories through the central character, Stephen; the reader ought to recall that Stephen is the name of one of Miranda's uncles (West *KAP* 29). The four-year-old Stephen refers, in his own mind, to his parents as "Mommanpoppa," their bedroom as "Mommanpoppasroom"; the Texas rural lingo continues in the child's innocent blasphemy when he baptizes (with illegal lemonade) the rose bush in "Name father son holygoat." Porter's humor is, needless to say, close at hand in this otherwise chilling story of child molestation.

As the title of this story suggests, the Edenic loss of innocence through disobedience leads, or *should lead*, to some sort of knowledge. The "downward path," the road of sin, beginning in small acts (like "stealing" sugar for lemonade and balloons for games) will supposedly lead to more serious misdemeanors later in life—or at least so goes the moralistic cant that Porter puts into the mouth of Stephen's Uncle David, an over-reacting pharisee, as the Grandmother, despite her peacemaking efforts, is the longsuffering sadducee.

As Sister M. Joselyn and others have observed, animal imagery plays an important role in this story. Stephen is described as a typical mammalian, desiring warmth and comfort: "He sank between his parents like a bear cub in a warm litter." When eating peanuts, he "crunches like a horse." His father thinks he is "dumb as an ox." When his parents indulge in their domestic arguments, their shrieking voices remind him of "the two tomcats who fought at night." Old Janet, the household servant, smells to him "like wet chicken feathers." And when at school he is given clay and told to make anything he wishes, he tries to make a cat, like Meeow, the household pet. All in all, life is a jungle, threatening, uncertain, mysteriously cruel. Most important, he stands "staring like an owl" when Mama and Papa are discussing his case; and like the owl (symbol of wisdom in this story about the downward path to such) he knows more than he seems to know. And his mother, when she attacks the hypocritical sermonizing of her relatives, refers to their "beastly little moral notions."

Knowledge in the biblical sense is subtly presented

in the ironic symbolic contexts of the story. Stephen is made to feel ashamed by Old Janet when she discovers that "there was a little end of him showing through the slit in his short blue flannel trousers." Profoundly self-conscious, "He felt guilty and red all over, because he had something that showed when he was dressed that was not supposed to show then." Even when he is bathed, the towels are wrapped quickly around him so that the body remains a hidden part of his nature. The description of the balloons as "limp objects," the licorice ("liquish," to Frances) as "the nice rubbery, twisty kind," and the treatment of the wet, lumpy clay—all these images point to unrealized, natural urges not yet visible in the four-year-old boy. Sin, misconduct in general, is associated with sexuality. Uncle David provides a clue to his own attitudes toward child rearing when he teaches the child to play at boxing, encouraging roughness. "We don't want him to be a sissy," he remarks. And in the name of the anti-sissification doctrine, it is clear that outright cruelty can be justified.

The four-year-old Stephen (modeled somewhat, no doubt, on Stephen Dedalus in Joyce's *A Portrait of the Artist as a Young Man*) falls from grace through his desire to please his playmate, the little girl, Frances. It is for her that he "steals" his uncle's advertising balloons and his Grandmother's lemon and sugar. Because of his father's alleged "bad blood," the child is seen as following in footsteps that run along "the downward path." "It's in the blood" is a favorite phrase of Stephen's tormentors.

That natural depravity is the curse under which Stephen lives is made manifest early in the story when Mama and Papa discuss his case. Papa says,

> "I suppose you'll say it's my fault he's dumb as an ox."

> "He's my little baby, my only baby," said Mama richly, hugging him, "and he's a dear lamb. . . . He's an angel and I'll never get used to having him."

> "We'd be better off if we never *had* had him," said Papa.

But they have had him. And this fact, Stephen's presence, is, it seems, the cause of the violent domestic arguments that cause Stephen to be bundled up and taken to his Grandmother's house every so often. In point of fact, Stephen is not "dumb as an ox"; he is quite clever when circumstances require him to be. And he is quite perceptive.

The story escapes sentimentality through the complete objectivity of tone. Stephen's mother, attacking with abandon the "beastly little moral notions" of her brother and her mother, might earn our

sympathy were it not for the evident fact that she is
in many ways an unfit mother, herself therefore un-
qualified to sermonize. And Stephen clearly does not
"like" either his parents or his uncle and grandmother, his surrogate parents. Bohemian abandon is
apparently as hurtful as Calvinistic rigidity to the
young child. Adding to the irony is—as usual in Porter's stories—the victim's unwitting cooperation
with his tormentors.

The story is told entirely from Stephen's point of
view, that of an innocent, helpless, naive child,
caught up in an unfriendly environment. The third-
person, "silent" narrator never intervenes to comment or interpret, except at one harmless point,
when the reader is told that Frances "was beginning
to feel that she had enough" lemonade. Even this
minor narrative flaw, if it is that, goes unnoticed by
the reader because Stephen quickly intuits this
truth for himself. The point of view otherwise remains as intact as any Jamesian could desire. Those
who have eyes to see do not see; and those who have
ears to hear do not hear. Those who have most to
learn, learn nothing. Irony blossoms all along the
way, as the downward path to wisdom leads, for the
adults, to a dead end. The story, which reminds us
clearly of James's "What Maisie Knew," can function as a Jamesian case study of child abuse. Without commentary or authorial intrusion, the objective

narrator pitilessly reports the facts. And the result is a powerful, detached reportage of "fallen" creatures seen through the eyes of a child, an "angel" entertained unawares among aliens.

"Noon Wine" (1936)

"Good country people" are examined in "Noon Wine," whose setting is a "small south Texas farm." Don Graham says that the story is set near Buda, Texas, very close to Kyle, the town where Katherine Anne Porter lived with her grandmother Porter (*Texas: A Literary Portrait*). In such small Texas towns and rural areas, respectability was all; what a man seemed to be was considerably more important, supposedly, than what he actually was. In fact, there inevitably arose a confusion between the seeming and the fact, so that one's genuine self was often lost in the social ideal. Don Graham has referred to *Noon Wine* as "the tragic story of a vain and foolish man named Royal Earle Thompson who destroyed himself because, in the Socratic sense, he did not know himself" (*Texas: A Literary Portrait* 64). And what keeps him from knowing himself is that he is so everlastingly concerned with what the neighbors will think of him. Like Mrs. Whipple in "He," Royal Earle Thompson could never look truly into himself.

But Southern respectability turns out not to be

valued at all by Katherine Anne Porter, any more
than it was by the early American Puritans or by
Nathaniel Hawthorne, under whose influence this
story partly was written. Significantly, the story is
set on a small farm in central Texas from 1896 to
1905, approximately the same period, as Hank Lopez points out, that Katherine Anne Porter herself
had lived in that region.

Mr. Royal Earle Thompson, as his name suggests,
is prone to take on "royal" airs when it comes to
domestic duties. His sorriness and lack of gumption
are typical of Porter's male characters. (One is
reminded that Porter once gave the nickname
"Hidalgo" to Miguel Covarrubias, her Mexican
lover, because he disliked domestic chores.) (Givner
KAP 194).

Katherine Anne Porter herself took pains to describe the inception of *Noon Wine* in her 1954 essay
"Noon Wine: The Sources." Every serious student of
Noon Wine should consult this essay, but each must
return to the text itself unclouded by the author's
intrusions if he or she is to grasp its significance.

The Thompsons, like the Whipples of "He," are
poor dirt farmers with very little going for them.
Mr. Thompson's laziness, sorriness, and rationalizations seem to offer little hope that the family will
ever be in much better circumstances. The farm is
neglected, maintenance practically unknown. The

reader accustomed to Southern regional fiction will be reminded of the "poor white trash" frequenting such works. And the sickly wife, Ellie, suffering from female troubles, is a stereotype needing little further elaboration.

But with the mysterious arrival of Mr. Helton the prospects of the Thompsons quickly improve. Mr. Helton demonstrates industry, frugality, and determination. Comically taking credit for Mr. Helton's improvements, Mr. Royal Earle Thompson now begins to move up in the world. Nothing darkens this idyllic picture except Mr. Helton's slight tendency toward violence when his personal belongings (especially his harmonicas, symbolizing his fragile personal and creative identity) are bothered by the Thompson children, Herbert and Arthur. The haunting melody played by Mr. Helton is suggestive of something mysterious, alien, but also something perhaps aesthetically attractive in him; Mr. Helton's ultimate destruction by this society can be metaphorically understood as the conservative community's need to destroy the threatening artist. Anyone raised under similar circumstances in such an atmosphere can readily understand this need. Even boys who took piano lessons in the rural areas were looked at askance during this period.

Mr. Thompson, essentially a no-account farmer, is enabled by Mr. Helton's industry to appear in the

social guise he prefers, something like a gentleman
farmer. We are informed ever so subtly that Mr.
Thompson is a drinking man, that he stops off at
"the hotel" in town for a nip whenever he has the
opportunity. It is clear throughout this story that
Mr. Thompson places an undue emphasis upon what
people will think, upon *reputation* as opposed to
character; this misplaced emphasis will be his destruction. For the Thompsons are like the Whipples;
having little of the world's goods, they tend to overrate the commodity that is most affordable, the
world's opinions.

Once again, Katherine Anne Porter paints a picture of a shiftless, passive, ineffectual male (like
that of her Texas father) wasting the family's resources. But in this story there is no dominant, take-
charge female to check such excesses. The marriage,
as a result, goes nowhere; it is static. Yet this marriage may be one of the more satisfactory ones in all
of Porter's fiction; so little is demanded of it that the
reader tends to assume its success. But Texas readers will understand easily that marriage in the context of economic hardship cannot be understood in
the same way that marriage amidst plenty can be
comprehended. Infidelity and divorce are luxuries,
having no place in the hardscrabble existence of the
Thompsons. It remains true, as many readers have
continually pointed out, that marriage does not

come off in a very good light in the fiction of Katherine Anne Porter.

With the arrival of Mr. Homer T. Hatch, all the chickens of this story come home to roost. Hatch is a most disgusting caricature of the financial opportunist, but he successfully cons Mr. Thompson into believing, in spite of himself, that something is amiss with Mr. Helton. To be more accurate, Mr. Thompson is afraid of what the neighbors will think if they learn that he is harboring an escapee from an insane asylum. The resulting violence is somewhat unexpected, but Mr. Homer T. Hatch suddenly lies killed. Mr. Thompson, who saw—or *thought* he saw, Mr. Hatch thrust a knife into Mr. Helton's stomach, splits open Mr. Hatch's head with an axe.

But Mr. Helton was *not* killed by Homer T. Hatch; he is hunted down and killed by a sheriff's posse. The knife that had *seemed* to go into his stomach actually never did. Mr. Thompson therefore has a problem: how is he to convince the neighbors (and the opinion of the neighbors is all-important to him) that his killing of the despicable Homer T. Hatch was in any way justified? It matters not at all to him that a good lawyer gets him off, for the court of public opinion has the final judgment. In the end, the only solution for Mr. Thompson is suicide, the only means whereby he can demonstrate his innocence.

Katherine Anne Porter's sympathetic under-

standing of the moral dilemma of Mr. Thompson is
vividly clear. But, ultimately, it seems that she
mocks, as usual, an excessive concern for what the
neighbors might think. The strong regional flavor of
the story can be easily demonstrated by Mr. Thompson's reaction to the redneck audience to whom he
addresses his pleas:

> . . . the two listening faces took on a mean
> look, a greedy, despising look, a look that said
> plain as day, "My, you must be a purty sorry
> feller to come round worrying about what *we*
> think, *we* know you wouldn't be here if you had
> anybody else to turn to—my, I wouldn't lower
> myself that much, myself." (*Collected Stories*
> 263)

Yet this is the very audience, the highest court, to
which Mr. Thompson must appeal. This story, like
"He," shows us that aspect of Texas rural life that
Katherine Anne Porter most hated, its preoccupation with the social order and its almost total obliteration of individuality. To be an individualist in
such a situation is almost impossible; conformity is a
requirement for the citizen who might at any time
have to call on his neighbors for assistance. This was
the very environment that Katherine Anne Porter
herself had to escape if she wanted a literary career.

In the preface to her *Collected Stories* (1965),
Katherine Anne Porter peevishly urged,

> Please do not call my short novels *Novelettes*,
> or even worse, *Novellas*. Novelette is classical
> usage for a trivial, dime-novel sort of thing;
> Novella is a slack, boneless, affected word that
> we do not need to describe anything. Please call
> my works by their right names: we have four
> that cover every division: short stories, long
> stories, short novels, novels. (vi)

Nevertheless, the proper term for works like *Noon Wine* is precisely *novella*, for it is this term that best describes the relationship between the novel and the short story form. The novella has a distinguished history in literature, and Katherine Anne Porter is one of its greatest practitioners. Porter's ultimate inability to write a successful full-length novel is instructive; if only she could be credited with having written "short novels," she could perhaps enter that select society of true literary folks. Yet it is only in the short fictional forms that Katherine Anne Porter is supreme. She would have done well to have avoided the novel altogether.

"Rope" (1928)

"Rope" is a comic masterpiece in the tradition of Washington Irving's "Rip Van Winkle" and James Thurber's "The Secret Life of Walter Mitty." The efficient, proud wife must deal with a passive, inef-

fectual male who cannot fulfill his masculine responsibilities and who therefore *must* be henpecked
if he is to amount to anything at all. The fact that it
is the female from whose point of view the story is
narrated is significant. The "rope" is both phalli-
cally symbolic and evocative of the umbilical cord
binding mother and child. The male in this story is
as useless as teats on a bull.

Although the setting is not made explicit, the
story has clear autobiographical references, and
"Rope" should be classified as a Texas story because
of its rural setting as well as its restatement of Porter's continual theme—the passive male (like Porter's Texas father) incapable of meeting domestic responsibility. The absolute unpredictability of love,
especially woman's love, is one of its themes. One
recalls Larry McMurtry's theft of the Texas cowboy's
aphorism—"A woman's love is like the morning
dew: it's just as apt to fall on a horseturd as it is on
a rose" (*In a Narrow Grave* 149). Though she might
not have worded the notion in quite this way,
Katherine Anne Porter was familiar with the sentiment.

The story no doubt owes much to Porter's rural
upbringing and knowledge of rural folklore. The
male is, of course, given enough "rope" to hang himself as far as his relationship with the female is concerned. One cannot help but be reminded of the folk

saying (popularized by Minnie Pearl on the Grand Ole Opry) about the man who—if you saw him coming down the road with a rope in his hand—you would not know whether he had lost a horse or found a rope.

"Magic" (1928)

"Magic" is set, like Part II of "Old Mortality," in New Orleans. Porter based the story on a tale she had heard from a New Orleans maid. What is most intriguing about the story as Porter finally presented it is, of course, the method of narration; the telling of the story determines the moral outlook of the tale. The story is, to put it punningly, a *telling* evocation of hypocritical moralizing.

Joan Givner describes the story in this way:

> It is a dramatic monologue by a maid who, hoping to relax her mistress as she brushes her hair, tells the story of a villainous madam who cheats and bullies the prostitutes in a New Orleans brothel. The point is that the madam's activity is made possible by those around her— the male clients, the police, the cook—who do nothing. Not only are these people as guilty as the one who perpetrates the violence but so too are the woman and the maid who relish the story. (*KAP* 197)

But Givner believes that "the point is not made sufficiently clear nor is it dramatized quite effectively, and the story, therefore, falls short of being a masterpiece." Indeed, most students of the story are baffled by it.

Givner's interpretation of the story is fine as far as it goes. It jibes with the stereotypical picture most of us have about "gossip at the hairdresser's." The callousness of Madame Blanchard, who apparently loves sordid gossip, is accounted for by her social position in relation to the maid; the tale of an unfortunate tart would not move her. But the story is much more complex than some critics will allow. The story is a double structure: (1) a story about a maid telling a story, and (2) a story told by a maid. What, then, is the relation of the two parts of the story? Are symmetrical patterns observable, as would be expected in a Porter story? Which part (1 or 2?) is predominant? Which character in the complex tale is the genuine protagonist? Finally, is there a moral other than the one pointed out by Givner—that people who do nothing about the injustices they are aware of are themselves guilty of injustice?

The most complete interpretation of the story to appear so far is Helen L. Leath's "Washing the Dirty Linen in Private: An Analysis of Katherine Anne

Porter's 'Magic'" (1985). Leath sees the story as one of those Porter tales of "strong women who struggle to control their environments, who use whatever means that present themselves in order to establish their dominion." For Leath, the maid-narrator is of central focus: "the narrator of 'Magic' uses a threat of magic spells to subjugate the mistress of the house and secure her job." Leath goes on to note that "Porter apparently admired women who were strong enough to survive, whether those women were Indian, French Negro, or East Texas transplants from Kentucky or Tennessee" (57). If the story is truly a "dramatic monologue," as has been suggested by several critics, then it follows—as Leath insists—that the reader must pay close attention to how the narrator reveals her own character and outlook, and not take in too literal a manner the actual "content" of the story told by the narrator. Indeed, the "unreliability" of narrators in the tradition of the dramatic monologue is notorious (Browning's narrators will come to mind). And the whole tradition of the tall tale in southwestern humor declares that it is the teller of the tale, not the tale, that is of foremost importance. Leath's argument is convincing simply because it fits the pattern of so much of Katherine Anne Porter's fiction. It seems, in addition, that critics have not been able to go beyond the black maid's station in life to the psychological complexities that she reveals in the story. The black maid is one of Porter's finest creations.

What many readers miss is the implied social criticism in this story. The maid-narrator of the frame story, as well as Ninette of the story proper, live "serenely" or "quietly." But living in serenity or quietness implies a loss of freedom, freedom being by its nature rambunctious and noisy. Both the maid and Ninette live under tyranny; the police are in cahoots with Ninette's persecutor, the entire social order in league with Madame Blanchard against the black maid, who apparently offers herself as a collaborator. All this economic exploitation works like "magic." But it is not "magic" that brings Ninette back to the brothel; it is the need for food and shelter. And it is not "magic" spells by which "the colored women" get back their men; unemployment and fatigue entice them back to their women who have, at best, subsistence-level domestic work that can offer them some small hope of survival. What is "magical" about all this is that an uprising to bring down the whole rotten system is not imminent. "Magically," the rotten system is perfumed over in gossip, small talk, and offers of collaboration. The "magic" is in the eye of the exploited only. Class warfare, not magic, keeps Ninette and the maid-narrator in line. And, like the stories in *The Old Order*, this narrative illustrates, once again, the absurdity of the Southern tradition that whites treated blacks with gentleness and tolerance. As Gaston has observed, "although the mistress is not so stereotyped as to harass the servant, she leaves no doubt about feeling vastly superior" (85).

"Magic" is the most "Marxist" of Katherine Anne Porter's stories. Remarkably, Marxist critics have not expounded this narrative. Indeed, Porter's leftist leanings during the early part of her career need scholarly attention. Her "Marxism" has never been fully discussed. Texas critics, living in a state in which even a liking for labor unions is considered subversive, have not found it convenient to examine this side of Katherine Anne Porter's early development. (One might also mention, at this point, the caricatured Marxism of Herr Müller in "Holiday," as well as the implied ironic treatment of Marxism in "Flowering Judas" and "Hacienda.") This story will, no doubt, elicit many more subtle interpretations. For one thing, clever critics will want to defend it against charges of vagueness, the vagueness being in the mind of the opposing and offending critics themselves. That the story is a *comic* creation, and that it bears relationships to the southwestern tall tale as well as to the dramatic monologue (the tall tale itself is a dramatic monologue), and that it presents a Marxist interpretation of the class strug-

gle—these are suggestions that should and will be
followed up.

"Holiday" (1960)

"Holiday" was composed, according to Katherine
Anne Porter herself, at least twenty-five years before it finally appeared in the December 1960 issue
of *The Atlantic* (*Collected Stories* v). The *Atlantic*
editor remarked in a headnote for the story: "In
Flowering Judas, her first and memorable collection
of short stories, and in *Pale Horse, Pale Rider*,
Katherine Anne Porter evoked some beautiful im-
pressions of the Southwest, a region which she knew
as a girl and which is very dear to her. To it she
returns in this new and exceptional narrative." Although the story was certainly not "new," there is no
doubt that it is "exceptional."

In the preface to the *Collected Stories* (1965), Porter informs the reader of the difficulties presented
by "Holiday":

> "Holiday" represents one of my prolonged
> struggles, not with questions of form or style,
> but my own moral and emotional collision with
> a human situation I was too young to cope with
> at the time it occurred; yet the story haunted
> me for years and I made three separate ver-
> sions, with a certain spot in all three where the

thing went off track. So I put it away and it disappeared . . . and I forgot it. It rose from one of my boxes of papers, after a quarter of a century, and I sat down in great excitement to read all three versions. I saw at once that the first was the right one, and as for the vexing question which had stopped me short long ago, it had in the course of living settled itself so slowly and deeply and secretly I wondered why I had ever been distressed by it. I changed one short paragraph and a line or two at the end and it was done. (v)

By calling detailed, though obscure, attention to "Holiday," Porter fashions a special place for it in the mind of the reader. This brief and rather vague explanation for the story's belated appearance functions as a "pre-text" or "bait" and is no doubt intended by Porter to lend an air of mystery to the text. Joan Givner has demystified the text for us, however, informing us of its association with Porter's first marriage to John Henry Koontz, a railroad employee who was stationed near the Louisiana border at one point in their marriage.

Significantly, "Holiday" is the only story other than "Hacienda" that is narrated by a first-person observer (DeMouy 166). The reason is most likely that Porter wished to soften the irony in both these narratives. The usual Porter narrator is highly ironic, "distanced," and ambivalent. What the first-person observer accomplishes is the removal of part of the "distance" between the narrator and the subject matter. In both "Holiday" and "Hacienda," Porter is writing about highly personal experiences. The narrator is, according to DeMouy, "an older Miranda than the one who experiences that rural Texas spring" (167). She has hindsight—wisdom gained through experience.

Winfred Emmons remarks that "'Holiday' is unique in that it is the only piece of Miss Porter's published writing that deals sympathetically with anything German" (34). But in truth Porter is at times anything *but* sympathetic with the "Germans" she describes in this story. And it is probably not Germans she is really describing at all, but rather the Swiss, associated with the family of her first husband, John Henry Koontz of Inez, Texas. When Porter scoffed at Texas Germans, she included the Swiss Koontzes in her scorn (Givner *KAP* 88). This fact may in part account for the ambivalent treatment of the "Germans" in this story. The "Germans" are certainly not evil as they are presented here; but neither are they particularly attractive. And their ability to suppress and exploit a family member who is mentally incompetent shows a side of their character that is at least ambivalently worrisome.

Emmons, writing before Givner's biography had

clarified this point, was at a loss to explain the setting for "Holiday":

> Exactly why Miss Porter placed the community near the Louisiana line, where in fact German settlement was sparse, is not clear; perhaps she felt that the lower half of extreme east Texas was more hurricane-prone than the regions of thicker German settlement, and she does work a storm into the story, though at the wrong season for hurricanes. (34)

From a strictly literary point of view, such considerations do not really matter. The slightly displaced setting and the stormy relationship with her first husband, a "foreigner" in Texas lingo, is the actual psychological background of the story.

Larry McMurtry's derogatory phrase, "East Texas pastoralism," designed to ridicule a certain type of nostalgic fictional treatment of a rather scruffy region, is *not* descriptive of this remarkable story.

The title of the story, "Holiday," has a double meaning. First, the narrator comes to this East Texas rural community to get away from the stress and strain of her work, to take a "holiday." Second, the narrator's attempt to provide Ottilie, the mentally retarded daughter of the Müllers, a "holiday" from the never-ending domestic drudgery provides an additional meaning of "holiday."

"Holiday" is thematically close in one sense to
"He." In Ottilie, the crippled cook, cleaner, scrubber,
general household drudge (a character not unlike
Mrs. Grimes in Sherwood Anderson's 1926 short
story "Death in the Woods"), the reader will recognize a human being similar to "Him" in the earlier
story. It is not until close to the end of the story that
the narrator even comes to recognize that Ottilie is
a family member, actually the oldest Müller daughter, who had been a completely normal child until a
crippling disease afflicted her at the age of five. Ottilie has been dehumanized and devalued by the
family because that is the only way they can justify
their continuing support of her on the farm. Thus,
ambivalence (one of Porter's favorite emotions) pervades the story. On the one hand, the reader is
shocked to see the debased condition of a family
member; on the other, one is puzzled by Ottilie's
acceptance of her debased condition. The love that
family members have for Ottilie has to be repressed
in order for Ottilie to have a chance at any form of
survival. Like Mrs. Whipple in "He," the family
have disguised and repressed their true feelings
about Ottilie. No other meaningful solution to their
dilemma suggests itself either to the family or to the
reader. In the difficult world of rural Texas, anyone
who is capable of work must work; and that work
must contribute to the good of the family unit. No
sentimental solution is viable.

The family unit is presented in this story in an ambivalent manner. Wives are the servants of their husbands, standing behind their chairs and serving them at mealtime. The patriarchal structure goes unquestioned. Yet love does abound, though not often articulated, between husbands and wives. Mr. Müller's weeping upon the death of his wife is shocking to the narrator. And Mr. Müller's Marxism (his only reading matter is a well-thumbed copy of *Das Kapital*) provides a comic incongruity; he strives to be a master in his household and in his community, and he believes that his "atheism" stands in the way of his rightful influence in the affairs of his region. In truth, no better example of the dedicated capitalist and communal conformist can readily be found in literature; yet Mr. Müller does, ironically, carry out Marx's intention through his interest in the well-being of the community.

Once again, Katherine Anne Porter has examined the life of the rural Texas community and found it wanting. The stifling of individuality at the expense of communal safety and security is what is seen as most threatening. Ottilie, then, can be seen at least in part as the symbol of what can happen to the individual who does not "fit" into the accepted scheme of things.

Texas readers will especially enjoy the magnificent descriptions of nature embedded in this story. "The deep blackland Texas farm country" is indeed one of the major actors in the dramatic situation. The changes of season, the garments worn by Mother Nature, the peasant fatalism growing out of the cycle of nature—all this will be appreciated by the regionalist critic. The landscape reinforces the conflicting emotions battling in the consciousness of the narrator:

> Winter in this part of the south is a moribund coma, not the northern death sleep with the sure promise of resurrection. But in my south, my loved and never-forgotten country, after her long sickness, with only a slight stirring, an opening of the eyes between one breath and the next, between night and day, the earth revives and bursts into the plenty of spring with fruit and flowers together, spring and summer at once under the hot shimmering blue sky. (*Collected Stories* 414)

And similar instances of "the pathetic fallacy" occur throughout the story. "Holiday" contains Porter's finest descriptions of nature.

"Holiday" represents one of Katherine Anne Porter's most strenuous efforts in the short story form. It is one of her most personal and intimate stories, dealing as it does with material that she would have preferred to banish from her consciousness. But everything comes together at last to produce a masterful piece of fiction. Arthur Voss in his history of *The American Short Story* remarks, with justice, that "'Holiday' is the work of a very great artist in fiction" (301).

Katherine Anne Porter's stories of the south and southwest rank as great literature under any standards, regional or aesthetic. And, as we have seen, it was her Texas upbringing that contributed most to these regional narratives.

4

STORIES OF MEXICO

The geographical proximity of Texas and Mexico played no small part in the literary career of Katherine Anne Porter. She first visited Mexico in 1920 and returned many times, both during and after the Obregón Revolution, a subject that was to become a persistent obsession in her fiction. As late as *Ship of Fools* (1962), Mexico and its complex social problems are on her mind. Often, on her Mexican trips, she would stop over in Texas either on the journey to or the return from Mexico. Porter's supposed "exile" from Texas during the years of her involvement with Mexican subjects is yet another myth demolished by Joan Givner's biography.

Beginning in 1921, and continuing over many years, Porter wrote a number of insightful analytical essays dealing with Mexico and its problems. Readers interested in this facet of Porter's career will want to consult her *Collected Essays and Occasional Writings* (1970). Porter described Mexico as "this sphinx of countries which for every fragment of authentic history yields two riddles" (Givner *KAP* 22). Some of her most engaging narratives are set here.

"María Concepción" (1922)

"María Concepción," though not, properly speaking, Porter's first published short story (she had published some children's stories previously), was certainly her first serious literary creation to see print. This story introduces a character type who is to dominate the fiction of Katherine Anne Porter: a strong-willed woman operating in a society of weak, ineffectual men. The evil to be eschewed is passivity, known to Porter through her whining, inactive, passive Texas father who, after the death of his wife, simply gave up and slowly withered away. María Concepción illustrates the power of a determined woman and, incidentally, it shows how a passive male can be dominated by such a determined woman.

"Instinctive serenity" marks María Concepción's character. She demonstrates that she is sufficient unto the day in her dealings within the community. Absolutely without sentimentality (like Katherine Anne Porter herself, except in her public image), María Concepción does what has to be done to preserve her place in the world.

When the pregnant María Concepción discovers her husband Juan, whom she had married in the Church, involved with María Rosa (the scarlet woman of the village) in an adulterous affair, she is outraged. After she is deserted by her husband and María Rosa (who leave together to fight in the Revolution), her baby is born dead. When Juan and María Rosa return to the village, María Concepción kills María Rosa with her butcher knife, taking María Rosa's infant to raise as her own, all this with the approval of the community. Her "instinctive serenity" has been restored. Porter concludes the story with a description of María Concepción and Juan in bed with the infant, after a difficult day:

> María Concepción could hear Juan's breathing . . . the house seemed to be resting after a burdensome day. She breathed, too, very slowly and quietly, each inspiration saturating her with repose. The child's light, faint breath was a mere shadowy moth of sound in the silver air. The night, the earth under her, seemed to swell and recede together with a limitless, unhurried, benign breathing. She drooped and closed her eyes, feeling the slow rise and fall within her own body. She did not know what it was, but it eased her all through. Even as she was falling asleep, head bowed over the child,

> she was still aware of a strange, wakeful hap-
> piness. (*Collected Stories* 21)

The heroine's method of dealing with the foulness
of the world (adultery and betrayal) was earlier fore-
shadowed in the story by her impassive treatment of
the chickens, "who twisted their stupefied eyes and
peered into her face inquiringly":

> María Concepción took the fowl by the head,
> and silently, swiftly drew her knife across its
> throat, twisting the head off with the casual
> firmness she might use with the top of a beet.

Further, María Concepción's determined refusal to
be beaten by her drunken husband (in contrast to
María Rosa, who submitted to such beatings from
Juan) marks María Concepción out as one of
Katherine Anne Porter's feminist heroines.

For Katherine Anne Porter personally, this
story—her first serious work of fiction to be accepted
by demanding critics—reveals an attitude toward
the world. She will henceforth do what is required to
achieve a rightful place in the world, and she will do
it with "instinctive serenity." As an active partici-
pant in the world, she will make short work of the
passive and the sentimental. The revenge motif is,
from a psychological point of view, aimed at her

Texas father and his whining incompetence. Katherine Anne Porter's "conception" of herself and of her literary art is, therefore, the genuine subject of "María Concepción."

"The Martyr" (1923)

Artistic creativity is also the apparent subject of "The Martyr." Were it not for its Mexican setting and the Spanish surnames, this story could almost have been lifted from Boccaccio's *Decameron*. A comic tale of unrequited love, it nevertheless posits a serious moral: each man martyrs himself for the things he loves—in Rubén's case an idealized woman primarily, tamales and pepper gravy secondarily; in aesthetic terms, sentimentality announces the death of art.

The story begins in the style of the conventional tale of the battle of the sexes:

> Rubén, the most illustrious painter in Mexico, was deeply in love with his model Isabel, who was in turn romantically attached to a rival artist whose name is of no importance.

Rubén is a painter like Reubens, a self-indulgent voluptuary, enraptured by the beauty of Isabel, who resembles Jezebel (Rubén's friends refer to her as a "lean she-devil"; and she may owe something to Is-

abel in Melville's *Pierre* (1852). It is clear from the
outset that Rubén/Reubens will lose in a contest
with Isabel/Jezebel. Isabel's pet name for Rubén,
"Churro," is, as the narrator is careful to tell us, "a
sort of sweet cake, and is, besides, a popular pet
name among the Mexicans for small dogs." Indeed,
Rubén is treated like a dog. And the more he is hu-
miliated by Isabel, the more he adores her. The gar-
gantuan self-pity exhibited by Rubén when he loses
his beloved Isabel to the rival artist is comically excessive. In personal terms, once again, Porter seems
to reject her father and the excessive grief that he
spent a lifetime nurturing.

Martyrdom is presented as a colossal expenditure
of psychic energy, leaving nothing left over for aesthetic production. When Isabel leaves him, the piti-
ful Rubén is without his inspiration and cannot continue to paint. The self-indulgent character of
martyrdom is symbolized by the ever-increasing
bulk of Rubén. His self-perpetuating disease must
be fueled by more and more sweet wine, cheese, and
tamales. It is fitting that Ramón, his ardent admirer
and prospective biographer, is a caricaturist, for
Rubén is pure stereotype, unadulterated romantic
fool who simply *must* die of nothing less than a bro-
ken heart, though in a café, and only after a massive
serving of tamales and pepper gravy, "his final in-
dulgence."

Food, as a substitute for sex, is patently served up
throughout the story. Ramón, the caricaturist, remarks that when his beloved Trinidad ("that shame-
less cheat-by-night") deserted him "nothing tasted
properly." In addition, he tells Rubén, he was struck
tone-deaf and color-blind. For Ramón, of course, such
a bland existence is only a temporary discomfort.
Rubén, on the other hand, cannot recover his interest in life. Sex has to be replaced by sugary red
wines and a spicy diet of tamales and pepper gravy.
But such a negative glorification of sex as the well-
spring of human life leads to death of the spirit and
a continually expanding physical bulk. His physi-
cian, a cynical realist in matters of this sort, recommends "a diet, fresh air, long walks, frequent violent
exercise, preferably on the cross-bar, ice showers,
almost no wine"—a litany unheard and unheeded by
Rubén.

Rubén is, of course, an ineffectual, passive male
weeping over a lost female (as Harrison Boone Porter wept for a lifetime over his dead wife). His inability or unwillingness to help himself or in any
way to shake off his lethargy is simply contemptible.
He fattens himself on a diet of sentimental claptrap,
and his friends collaborate, because of their "deli-
cacy," in the consequent and literal breaking of his
heart.

Darlene Unrue has pointed out that "Martyr" has

as its context the real-life relationship between Diego Rivera and his first wife, Guadalupe Marin (*Understanding KAP* 29–30). Porter's detachment concerning Rivera's revolutionary murals accounts for the ironic tone of this story.

"Virgin Violeta" (1924)

"Virgin Violeta" describes erotic awakenings in an adolescent girl. Violeta, almost fifteen years old, is a fragile, lovely flower; a virgin, convent educated, now beginning to blossom into young womanhood. Because "Virgin Violeta" is more a character sketch than a story, very little happens in the narrative, and Violeta is intended as rather a gentle caricature than a heroine. The charm of this sketch lies in contemplation of Violeta's erotic yearnings which she passionately *feels* but does not quite *understand*. The essential conflict in the narrative is in the mind of Violeta herself; she burns to be ravished, but she is profoundly afraid of sex.

The implied criticism of the Catholic Church and its cult of virginity is kept quietly in the background, as unobtrusive as the "small painting on the white-paneled wall . . . 'Pious Interview between the Most Holy Virgin Queen of Heaven and Her Faithful Servant St. Ignatius Loyola' . . . there was nothing to stare at." It is altogether fitting that she

makes "ugly caricatures of her cousin Carlos" after
her unnerving experience with him (amounting to
nothing more than a stolen kiss); she is herself a
caricature. The "violet" virgin, all too close to the
"violated" virgin in our uneasy linguistic consciousness, is framed gently by a master caricaturist. If
Porter had been a painter instead of a writer of tales
and sketches, this sketch might be called "Portrait
of the Virgin."

"Flowering Judas" (1930)

"Flowering Judas," considered by many critics one
of the greatest of American short stories, and by
most Porter critics as her finest production in that
genre, appears in all major American short story
collections. In this story, for a change, it is the female who is passive (it would seem), the male dominant (after a fashion), though it can be seen that
Laura's passivity is in this case a survival strategy
and is very close in fact to dominance.

In her role as a revolutionary, Laura is the passive
being in a man's world, both consciously and unconsciously catering to the world of masculine urges to
power and dominance; thus she is a "Judas" figure
in full bloom as the story unfolds. Her fear of Braggioni, in reality her fear of obliteration, causes her
to cater to his smallest wishes—except his desire for

sexual relations, that sacrifice apparently reserved as a last resort to protect her life. As long as she can say "No" to sexuality, so long does she have something of value that can be bartered for her continued existence. That Laura may eventually be required to surrender even her sexual integrity to Braggioni is strongly suggested in Porter's masterful use of the pistol (a transparent phallic symbol), which Laura is required to clean and polish, and which Braggioni strokes, ever so gently, while it lies in her lap. Reinforcing the theme of the inevitable sexual surrender of Laura to Braggioni is her willingness to listen to Braggioni's singing, despite the fact that she is bored to tears, while he "curves his swollen fingers around the throat of the guitar and softly smothers the music out of it" and "scratches" a miserable melody from the instrument, a foreshadowing of the inevitable rape/violation/seduction awaiting her, a consummation, however, that may not necessarily spell her destruction. The counterplay of pistol and guitar set the threatening, ominous stage; but Laura is something of a stage manager. As the desirable female, yet a woman traitorous to conventional womanhood, power lurks in her being. While nothing good is promised for Laura, and though her passivity assures her continued desirability, she treads a dangerous course.

Laura's essential treason is that she is being *used*

for the purpose of others; she is not actively or passionately *engaged* in the revolutionary enterprise.
Like the original Judas, she has sold out. She is not
really Catholic, only Catholic in name, but she
knows how to manipulate the trappings and symbolic rigmarole of the Church (like any good creative
artist who finds Catholic symbol more useful than
barren Protestant motif). She is not *really* aristo-
cratic, but a desire for lace that is not machine-made
suggests that she aims at standards for herself that
she would not struggle to achieve for others; here
she resembles the erotic Braggioni who loves his yel-
low silk handkerchiefs, "Jockey Club, imported from
New York." Her Marxism, like that of Braggioni, is
purely for show; it is a way to walk within the cor-
ridors of power. She, like Braggioni, proves quite
capable of administering the death penalty; like the
survivor that she essentially is, she will continue on
this dangerous path.

Laura, as Joan Givner has shown, is in a predicament quite close to the situation faced by Katherine Anne Porter while she was in Mexico during the
Revolution. Laura is not named "Miranda" for a variety of reasons, but "Flowering Judas" is in a sense
a "Miranda story"; for this story describes a spiritual
crisis in Porter's alter-ego. The problem is how to
remain true to oneself and at the same time achieve
status in the world; to keep the faith and yet survive

to go on working for a cause that promises both danger and excitement for oneself. To surrender the faith that others are dying for is despicable; to die for a cause may be a noble act, but scarcely noted by those engaged in such brutal struggles. All these considerations did, no doubt, enter into the composition of "Flowering Judas," the story that, more than any other, reveals Katherine Anne Porter's absolute self-confidence.

Harold Bloom believes that "Flowering Judas" is really concerned with Porter's intense desire to become an artist of the first rank, a necessarily narcissistic impulse displaced, in the fictional narrative, as a conflict between loyalty to the world and loyalty to the spirit.

> Porter's story, intensely erotic, is neither a "Waste Land" allegory, nor a study of Christian nostalgia. Its beautiful, sleep-walking Laura is neither a betrayer nor a failed believer, but an aesthete, a storyteller poised upon the threshold of crossing over into her own art. (*Modern Critical Views* 2)

Quoting the Freudian view of narcissism as a feminine strategy for dominance, Bloom observes, with Freud, that "the importance of this type of woman for the erotic life of mankind must be recognized as very great" (2). The feminine self-sufficiency that such a woman feels, the thrill of power over others is preliminary, in Freud's view, to acts of dominance. Feeling no need to love, their desire is *to be loved*; and being loved is a sure path to power over those who love. Laura as teacher demonstrates the same characteristics; her childish pupils attempt to express love for their "titcher," but she holds them at arm's length. Conventional masculine readers will, no doubt, recognize Laura's behavior as "bitchiness"; female readers, responding to Braggioni as an "SOB," will be more sympathetic with her plight and with the strategy she finds it necessary to adopt for survival. The idolatrous image of success, whether erotic, political, or aesthetic, is—after all— a "bitch-goddess" for the ambitious, both male and female. Laura's most important character trait is the same as that of María Concepción—"instinctive serenity." The story of Laura (the quest for the laurel) involves a conflation of Judas tree and laurel tree; it is a story of treason to the world for the purpose of loyalty to the integrated self.

Laura's need to be in the company of Braggioni (the braggart), master of men, and yet to resist his appeals can be interpreted as a power play in itself. Laura's "treason" in this sense is that she is serving herself instead of a cause; but, of course, such "treason" is what most revolutionaries are guilty of.

Braggioni speaks truly when he tells Laura that "We are more alike than you realize in some things."

Laura's dream at the conclusion of the story has been interpreted variously. Clearly, the dream constitutes Laura's recognition of her situation. Bloom provides the following analysis:

> The dream-vision that ends the story is hardly a representation of a dream, since it is anything but a wish-fulfillment. It is the narcissist's ultimate reverie, an image of the Judas tree representing not betrayal so much as a revelation that the flowering Judas is oneself, one's perfect self-sufficiency. (3)

If Bloom is correct, what we have in "Flowering Judas" is Katherine Anne Porter's announcement to the world that "the little girl from Texas" has arrived on the scene and must be wrestled with. Porter's weapon in her struggle for status is the same as Laura's in her resistance to Braggioni: "the consoling rigidity of the printed page."

Critics have pointed out, in numerous studies, the many levels of Christian imagery present in the text. Supplication (the washing of feet), the offering of food (communion), the asking for forgiveness (supplication), the relief to be gained from tears (baptism), the return of Eugenio, after death, to Laura in her dreams (resurrection), Eugenio (etymologically "well born") as savior (or false savior), and Laura's understanding that she cannot equate love and revolution (repentance)—all readers will continue to enjoy the richness of symbol and image in this story. The relationship between Braggioni and Laura can be seen as a perversion of the relationship between saint and savior. It is not likely that formalist critics will soon lose interest in the Christian imagery of "Flowering Judas."

"Hacienda" (1932, 1934)

"Hacienda" originally appeared in a shorter version in the *Virginia Quarterly Review*. The 1934 version, subtly revised, thoroughly expanded, and completely rethought, deserves a better critical reception than it has thus far received. It belongs in the short story genre, though some critics (Arthur Voss, for example) consider it a short novel. The story is soundly based on Porter's keen observation of Mexican culture; she had actually visited the hacienda where Sergei Eisenstein was attempting to film his ill-fated and abortive epic, *Que Viva Mexico*. Penetrating, pitiless observation and journalistic objectivity in reportage of scene characterize this major achievement.

The setting of "Hacienda" is Mexico in 1929. The

story is—as Edward Simmen aptly describes it—"a brilliantly complex portrayal of the generally negative results of the 1910 revolution seen at every level of Mexican society" (xxxvii). Although the intent of the story seems clearly to describe conditions in 1929, some readers will not consider the story "dated," since similar conditions exist even today. Simmen notes these conditions described in the story which can be seen in Mexico:

> the staggering poverty on the one hand and the enormous wealth on the other; the corruption that grows out of the bureaucratic snarls which end only with inevitable bribes to the appropriate official; the strictly drawn social boundaries; the intensity of life at every level of society; as well as the sense, sensibility and humor of the Mexican people. (xxxviii)

The betrayal of the common people (the Mexican Indians, in this case), their aspirations and dreams, by the victors in the Revolution is ironically presented. The plot concerns Americans and Russians making a motion picture in a Mexican border town. Although generally considered weaker than Porter's more famous stories with Mexican settings, "Flowering Judas" and "María Concepción," it is, in its Jamesian way, a masterpiece of setting. It is not surprising, perhaps, that Edward Simmen, editor of the 1987 anthology *Gringos in Mexico*, dealing with the American literary experience in Mexico from the years 1872 to 1983, should have included "Hacienda" as the book's representative Porter text rather than the more famous examples of Porter's Mexican fiction. For there is in this story a powerful representation of the inability of foreigners to understand Mexican culture; the gringos (Americans, Russians, whoever) who gaze upon Mexico simply remain *unaware*. The Jamesian injunction, "Try to be one of those on whom nothing is lost," is lost upon all gringos concerned, perhaps even the narrator.

But if the story is Jamesian in its ironic detachment, it is Whitmanian in its celebration of nature. Consider, for example, the Whitmanian catalogue of natural cleanliness, the narrator's silent rebuke of a gringo who prides himself on Anglo-Saxon cleanliness:

> Some day I shall make a poem to kittens washing themselves in the mornings; to Indians scrubbing their clothes to rags and their bodies to sleekness, with great slabs of sweet-smelling strong soap and wisps of henequen fiber, in the shade of trees, along river banks at midday; to horses rolling sprawling snorting rubbing themselves against the grass to cleanse their healthy hides; to naked children shouting in pools; to hens singing in their dust

baths; to sober fathers of families forgetting
themselves in song under the discreet flood of
tapwater; to birds on the boughs ruffling and
oiling their feathers in delight; to girls and
boys arranging themselves like baskets of fruit
for each other: to all thriving creatures making
themselves cleanly and comely to the greater
glory of life. (*Collected Stories* 138–39)

Could Walt Whitman have put it better? It is true
that in conversation Porter often contrasted Whit-
man-minded writers and James-minded writers and
was careful to include herself among the Jamesians
(Unrue *Understanding KAP* 13); but a virtuoso artist can take aesthetic ideology only so far. In this
area, as well as in many others, Porter has misled
her critics. Lopez quotes her as saying that "the influence of Whitman on certain American writers
has been disastrous, for he encourages them in the
vices of self-love (often disguised as love of humanity, or the working classes, or God)" (228–29). But it
is exactly that type of self-love which characterizes
much of Porter's own fiction, and which she wishes
to disguise in order to conform to notions implanted
in her by the New Critics.

It may be that "Hacienda" was the genesis for
Ship of Fools (1962). The introductory section of that
novel, with its viciously ironic presentation of the
sordid conditions in Veracruz, certainly recalls sim-

ilar conditions described by Porter some twenty-eight years earlier in the short story.

In "Hacienda" we see a great virtuoso exhibiting her impressive technical skills.

"That Tree" (1934)

"That Tree" describes American journalists living temporarily in Mexico. The journalists are a kind of plague to the Mexican natives—a swarm of parasites who consume their resources, and look down their noses at their "primitive" culture. Porfirio Diaz is reputed to have said, "Poor Mexico! So far from God and so close to the United States." The closeness of Mexico to the United States has, in fact, been one of its major problems. The American curse that materialized in the form of parasitic journalists who swarmed over the nation during the Obregón Revolution to "interpret" Mexican culture for their readers is the context of this story. Porter herself was, of course, one of the breed. As a presumed authority on things Mexican, she was offered numerous journalistic assignments that required her presence in Mexico.

The journalist, a male chauvinist pig if ever there was one, and almost totally without redeeming social value, had come to Mexico without a truly noble cause in view:

He had really wanted to be a cheerful bum lying under a tree in a good climate, writing poetry. He wrote bushel basketsful of poetry and it was all no good and he knew it, even while he was writing it. . . . He would have enjoyed just that kind of life; no respectability, no responsibility, no money to speak of, wearing worn-out sandals and a becoming, if probably ragged, blue shirt, lying under a tree writing poetry. (*Collected Stories* 66)

But he has difficulty in finding that ideal tree, under which he can write poetry and do little else except imbibe the local alcoholic beverages. It is his wife, Miriam (named, no doubt, for the sister of Moses the lawgiver), who casts a pall over all this useless activity.

She is a Midwestern schoolteacher, a virgin with no interest in sexual experimentation, and a genuine desire to get ahead in the world. The anti-hero of the tale loses his job, becomes a parasite upon his wife, and suffers the indignity of a divorce. But her leaving at last instills in him a will to succeed in journalism, which he does. Renouncing art (no great sacrifice, since his talent was non-existent), he rises in the world. When, five years later, his former wife asks to come back, he is willing to take her on his own terms, or so he drunkenly tells himself.

An ineffectual, alcoholic, passive male in confrontation with a dominant female who goads him into action (suggestive, as usual, of Porter's Texas father and her Texas paternal grandmother) form the core of the tale. The male, who drifts from one relationship to another (he has an affair with an Indian woman while corresponding with his wife), and cannot manage even the simplest of household chores, is given sufficient scope in this tale to reveal himself as a cad, a bum, and a shiftless, sorry good-for-nothing, when all is said and done. The reader is exasperated with his passivity, as no doubt Katherine Anne Porter was exasperated with all such masculine types.

The style of the story is Hemingway-burlesque. Everything takes place within a bar, and not exactly "a clean, well-lighted" bar. All is reminiscence narrated by a third-person ironic observer. The "tough-guy" speeches spoken by barroom brawlers evoke the worst aspects of the wasted life of expatriates.

On a personal basis, Katherine Anne Porter seems in this story to be working out the proper self-attitude towards her career in Mexican journalism. The self-criticism is pitiless; called into question is the whole notion of whether she can be an artist or whether she must remain a bum journalist, a parasite in a foreign country. The moralistic side of Porter's thought (represented by the shrewish Miriam in the narrative) is dominant here. Here

Porter renounces caricatured notions of art-for-art's-sake and the spiritual notion of the artist. It has become clear to her that all human beings, artists included, are looking out for the main chance. Journalism is rejected; genuine artistic creativity (which involves hard work, responsibility, dedication, sobriety, commitment, and all the other elements of the Mosaic code) are now embraced.

Mexico and its problems were to remain important to Katherine Anne Porter. Even as late as *Ship of Fools* (1962), she was preoccupied with the land "south of the border."

5

STORIES OF NEW YORK AND NEW ENGLAND

Katherine Anne Porter's stories of New York and New England are not important for their treatment of the "local color" of those geographic areas. In these stories, Porter is concerned with the same themes, character types, and situations that can be found in the remainder of her fiction. The setting is therefore not a major consideration of this group of narratives. She continues to be a Texas writer who happens to be writing, or pretending to write, about other areas of the country.

"Theft" (1929)

"Theft" has been called by Willene and George Hendrick "a perfect story" that "unmercifully lays bare the conflict between myth and reality" (65). Porter's life in New York City comes into play in this tightly constructed narrative which functions as an urban "slice of life." The heroine's stolen purse provides the basis for an examination of her character; weighed in a moral balance, the heroine finds that she, as a victim of theft, is in part responsible for theft. Criminal and victim are in collusion.

Porter's rural Texas habits are in evidence in this tale. The nameless heroine, obviously a young woman very much like Katherine Anne Porter herself, never locks doors; she leaves things lying carelessly around; she puts a trust in the natural goodness of her associates and acquaintances, and even brags to her friends about her careless habits. But being "a little girl from Texas in New York" imposes certain unpleasant truths upon her consciousness. A person willing to be taken advantage of *will be* taken advantage of in this dog-eat-dog milieu.

The female protagonist is by nature passive (always a serious moral flaw in Porter's world), one who does not want to make a scene. The moral seems clear: the passive individual is victimized because she allows herself to be victimized; the victimization occurs *because* the victim cooperates with the victimizer. While one might consider the heroine noble in one respect (she is above making an issue of petty theft), one must also consider her culpable in another respect: her failure to resist crime is an encouragement of crime. Weakness invites attack; passivity is a cause of violence. Once again, Katherine

Anne Porter launches an attack against the unforgivable sin of her Texas father—passivity, refusal to be bothered, lack of interest in the moral issues involved in any given situation, a dislike of being hassled, a desire not to get involved. Interestingly, Porter never had any difficulty in condemning her father for such weaknesses of character; in this story, Porter's alter-ego faces up to the same deficiencies in her own character.

When her purse, a special gift, is stolen, obviously by a janitress, the heroine accosts the janitress and demands the purse back. When the janitress finally admits the theft, however, the tables are turned. The janitress now accuses *the victim* of thievery; for, as it turns out, the janitress has a niece who really "needs" the purse much worse than its legal owner. The janitress had been encouraged in the theft because of the careless way that things had been left lying around in the apartment. "It's not from me, it's from her you're stealing it," the janitress says.

The heroine understands, finally, that "I was right not to be afraid of any thief but myself, who will end by leaving me nothing." In fact, the story is a compound of several examples of how the protagonist allows herself to be taken advantage of. Rather than take up arms against her tormentors, however, her usual response is simply "Let it go."

The Joycean epiphany is vintage Porter:

> In this moment she felt that she had been robbed of an enormous number of valuable things, whether material or intangible: things lost or broken by her own fault, things she had forgotten and left in houses when she moved: books borrowed from her and not returned, journeys she had planned and had not made, words she had waited to hear spoken to her and had not heard, and the words she had meant to answer with; bitter alternatives and intolerable substitutes worse than nothing, and yet inescapable: the long patient suffering of dying friendships and the dark inexplicable death of love—all that she had had, and all that she had missed, were lost together, and were twice lost in this landslide of remembered losses.

The clear, spare prose describes the heroine's sense of futility in her human relationships. She has repeatedly been betrayed. And she is herself responsible for these betrayals. The only thief she has to fear is herself. Passivity and indifference in human relations are open invitations to the world's opportunists.

Joan Givner has shown how Katherine Anne Porter came to believe that practically all her associates tried in some way to exploit her (*KAP* 207). "Theft" is a particularly frightening picture of the way a woman like Katherine Anne Porter could allow (unconsciously encourage) her friends to exploit her.

"The Cracked Looking-Glass" (1932)

"The Cracked Looking-Glass" takes place in rural Connecticut and New York City. Like "A Day's Work" (1940), it is a story about the Irish.

Rosaleen and Dennis O'Toole have been married for twenty-five years, and it seems clear that they deserve each other. The fact that he is thirty years older than she has only recently become anything of a problem for her. His impotence is accepted, but Rosaleen reminisces about Dennis as a younger man, when he was a headwaiter at a fashionable New York restaurant. Advancing age has caused him to be shiftless and passive, sexually impotent, and constantly in the way when chores are to be done. (Once again, the passive, ineffectual male—resembling Porter's Texas father—interacts with a female willing to take charge.) Rosaleen's vague, unrealized sexual urges are now unconsciously directed to traveling salesmen, neighborhood teenagers, and a local Irish ruffian named Hugh Sullivan, whose sly passes she resents. Kevin, a young man of the village, who left for New York after a quarrel with her, was young enough to be her son, but she

later comes to realize that erotic yearnings were not
altogether absent from his mind.

After a misbegotten journey to visit her sister
Honoria in Boston (though she travelled by way of
New York), where she encountered an Irish lad with
a dirty mind, she is happy to return to Connecticut,
to her old husband, and to the comforts of her domestic arrangement. As the story ends, the reader is
given to understand that things will go well from
now on. The marriage is a stable one; neither part-
ner could, after all, do much better.

Porter's Protestant upbringing in rural Texas
comes into play in this story, as does her subsequent
aesthetic preference for Roman Catholicism. On one
occasion, in her musings, Rosaleen wishes that
things could have been different, that she and her
husband had never come to Connecticut,

> where there was nobody to talk to but Roo-
> shans and Polacks and Wops no better than
> Black Protestants when you come right down
> to it. And the natives were worse even. A pic-
> ture of the neighbors up the hill came into her
> mind: a starved-looking woman in a blackish
> gray dress, and a jaundiced man with red-
> rimmed eyes, and their mizzle-witted boy. On
> Sundays they shambled by in their sad old
> shoes, walking to the meeting-house, but that
> was all the religion they had, thought Rosa-

> leen, contemptuously. On week days they beat
> the poor boy and the animals, and fought be-
> tween themselves. Never a feast-day, nor a bit
> of bright color in their clothes, nor a Christian
> look out of their eyes for a living soul. (*Col-
> lected Stories* 107–8)

The barrenness of the Protestant faith, contrasted
with the poetic richness of Catholicism is, of course,
vintage Porter.

Another interesting facet of "The Cracked Looking-Glass" is its depiction of a marriage in which the
age difference is thirty years. By internal evidence,
Dennis married when he was almost fifty; the
twenty-fifth wedding anniversary makes him sev-
enty-five years old; Rosaleen, whom we know to be
thirty years younger, is therefore forty-five years old
as the narrative unfolds. Katherine Anne Porter's
own penchant for younger men, and her understanding of the poignancy of such relationships, supplies a
psychological context for this narrative. The story,
in fact, seems almost a prefiguring of her marriage,
in 1938, to Albert Erskine (twenty-one years her
junior). Erskine, who was twenty-seven years old at
the time, and Porter, who was forty-eight, experi-
enced a relationship similar in some ways to the
characters in this story.

The central symbol of the story, the cracked looking-glass, functions as a device for Rosaleen to re-

flect upon her present situation and the strange ways by which she has come to it. The fact that she forgets to purchase another looking-glass while on her abortive journey bodes well for the continued marriage relationship. The glass, as Dennis remarks, is "a good enough glass." So with the marriage: it is "good enough."

In "The Cracked Looking-Glass," Porter looks through a glass darkly at the married state, its threats and promises. Marriage, never idyllically presented by Porter, seems in this case to be not the worst situation for the pair involved.

From the standpoint of technique, "The Cracked Looking-Glass" is a masterful tale involving constant shifts in point of view. Porter's intention, apparently, is to inform the reader of the attitudes of each of the partners toward this strange marriage. Consequently, it is not really through dialogue (which tells us very little here) but through the reportage of the inner thoughts of each of the partners in turn (not shared with the other, of course) that the full portrait of the marriage is rendered. Point of view shifts admirably at just the right points in the story.

It is probable that Porter's longing for home, her distrust of foreigners, and her sense of alienation supplied much of the tone of this story about the Irish of New York and Connecticut; the tale was composed in Mexico City and Berlin in 1931. That part of the characterization that is most suggestive of Katherine Anne Porter personally is Rosaleen's storytelling "lies." These lies are certainly *that*; but they prove to be lies that give shape and substance to an otherwise bleak existence. Rosaleen's age is approximately the same as Katherine Anne Porter's at the time this story was written.

"A Day's Work" (1940)

"A Day's Work" is, like the 1932 story "The Cracked Looking-Glass," a narrative dealing with the Irish. It treats of the poverty and misery of the poor Irish in New York during the Depression of the 1930s. It is an unflinching study of a miserable marriage and of the two miserable human beings caught up in it. Porter wrote the story as a result of conversations overheard in the air vent of her Perry Street apartment in New York City (Givner *KAP* 303). It comes as close to "Naturalism" as anything Porter was ever to write. The story depicts Porter's favorite thematic material—a sorry, unemployed, indecisive, passive husband attempting to deal with a necessarily shrewish wife who, he thinks, keeps him from advancing up the ladder of success. The story owes much to the marriage of Katherine Porter and Eugene Pressly which was breaking up at the time the story was composed, during the spring of 1937. Pressly's indecisiveness about his future and his constant interference with her creative work had caused the failure of the seven-year marriage.

The brutal beating scene at the conclusion of this story was probably psychological relief for Katherine Anne Porter, who, as usual, was able in her fiction to punish the exasperatingly passive male who (like her father) unwittingly caused great human suffering for all those connected with him. The reader will also, no doubt, compare this scene with the beating, in *Ship of Fools*, administered to William Denny, the drunken Texan, by Mrs. Treadwell. The clinical perspective attained by Porter in "A Day's Work" reveals a profound psychological intensity, which raises it somewhat above a naturalistic "case study." What is happening is that Porter is vicariously brutalizing all the passive, ineffectual males that have interfered with her work. The beating scene is sufficient to illustrate this principle:

> When the door was shut and locked, Mrs. Halloran went and dipped a large bath towel under the kitchen tap. She wrung it out and tied several good hard knots in one end and tried it out with a whack on the edge of the table. She walked in and stood over the bed and brought the knotted towel down in Mr. Halloran's face with all her might. He stirred and

muttered, ill at ease. "That's for the flatiron,
Halloran," she told him, in a cautious voice as
if she were talking to herself, and whack, down
came the towel again. "That's for the half-dol-
lar," she said, and whack, "that's for your
drunkenness—" Her arm swung around regu-
larly, ending with a heavy thud on the face
that was beginning to squirm, gasp, lift itself
from the pillow and fall back again, in a puzzled kind of torment. "For your sock feet," Mrs.
Halloran told him, whack, "and your laziness,
and this is for missing Mass and"—here she
swung half a dozen times—"that is for your
daughter and your part in her."

But lest the sentimental reader be tempted to sym-
pathize with the overburdened Mrs. Halloran, Porter is careful to reveal her self-righteousness and
her pettiness. Going to the telephone, she calls her
daughter so that she can moralize just a bit:

"Is that you, Maggie? Well, are things any
better with you now? I'm glad to hear it. It's
late to be calling, but there's news about your
father. No, no, nothing of that kind, he's got a
job. I said a *job*. Yes, at last, after all my urging
him onward. . . . It's clean enough work, with
good pay; if it's not just what I prayed for, still
it beats nothing, Maggie. After all my trying
. . . it's like a miracle. You see what can be done

> with patience and doing your duty, Maggie.
> Now mind you do as well by your own hus-
> band."

This passage is even more effective because at this
point the story comes to an abrupt end. The reader is
left with this final view of Mrs. Halloran. The fact
that Mr. Halloran's "job" will be political hack work
and may involve his making the rounds of taverns,
the seeking of bribes, and so on—all this is rational-
ized away in order that she can demonstrate to her
daughter the value of persistence in a miserable
marriage. The institution of marriage, in this story,
is exactly what Byron called it in *Don Juan*—"holy
deadlock."

6

STORIES OF GERMANY: "THE LEANING TOWER" AND *SHIP OF FOOLS*

We have already observed, in the chapter dealing with the stories of Texas, the South, and the Southwest, that Katherine Anne Porter's impressive story "Holiday," published in 1960 but written many years earlier, ostensibly deals with German settlers in East Texas; but in reality this narrative is her imaginative treatment of a family of Swiss descent, associated in her mind with the affairs of her first husband, John Henry Koontz, who once worked as a railroad employee along the Texas/Louisiana border. Some critics, like Winfred Emmons, rejoiced over that story because it seemed that for once Porter had treated "Germans" in a sympathetic light (34). But such is not the case.

Although Porter does, for whatever reason, refer to "Germans" and the German community in "Holiday," it seems clear that this story belongs in the category of stories about Texas, the South, and the Southwest—not in the category of stories about Germany. But just for the record, one *must* note that the characters in "Holiday"—German, Swiss, Texan, or whatever—are not invariably treated in a sympathetic light. There is no Porter narrative, in fact, in which Germans are treated in a very sympathetic manner; indeed it is doubtful that any individual German character in her work is described in a sympathetic manner.

Exactly why Germans were so loathsome to Katherine Anne Porter is a matter of speculation. Joan Givner's biography supplies some helpful information in this regard. Porter's upbringing among dirt-poor Texas farmers close by to certain prosperous German farmers is perhaps one clue. Another motivation is perhaps her close lifelong friendship with Erna Schlemmer (later Erna Glover Johns), a Kyle native and daughter of a prosperous German merchant who engaged seventeen employees; the contrast between Erna's upbringing in affluence and her own in poverty perhaps unconsciously affected Katherine Anne Porter. Another clue is the close relationship that Porter had with certain high-ranking Nazis during her period of residence in Germany in the fall of 1931. It may be that hindsight, the one truly exact science, taught Katherine Anne Porter the folly of agreement with so unpopular a cause as that of the German Nazis. Perhaps, for reasons of prudence, she used overkill in hiding any traces of pro-German sentiment; the only real trace of such sentiment being an anti-Semitism that surfaces on various occasions in *Ship of Fools* and "The Leaning Tower."

"The Leaning Tower" (1941)

"The Leaning Tower" is a story very much in the Jamesian tradition, depicting the American in Europe. But the story as Porter presents it is quite different from anything that Henry James could have managed. Porter never lets us forget that her narrative concerns *a Texan* in Berlin; and his moral sense is judged to be superior (though perhaps ineffective because of his passivity) to that of the Germans.

The setting is Berlin of 1931, the capital of a nation defeated in World War I; a nation whining over its defeat, now in the throes of a desperate financial inflation, unemployment, poverty, grimly accepting a steadily more menacing police state, greedy for the essentials of life, steadily preparing for the next war, ripe for a messiah. When Charles Upton (the Texan gone "uptown") goes into a barbershop to have his hair styled, he sees a photograph of "a little shouting politician, top lock on end, wide-stretched mouth adorned by a square mustache, who had, apparently, made the style popular." Adolph Hitler, style setter, is thus put in his place with consummate Porterian irony.

The central symbol of the story, the plaster model of the Leaning Tower of Pisa, functions on many levels but chiefly to illustrate the precarious state of Western civilization; at any moment it can come crashing down all around us. Human relationships, likewise, crumble at the slightest sign of strain. Economic relations are corrupted. Distrust reigns everywhere. Human life, symbolized by the many images of animals and animal life, has become degraded and something less than truly human.

The central character of the story, Charles Upton—because of his West Texas origin—is probably to be thought of as allied with the Miranda stories (West *KAP* 31). Charles Upton had come to Berlin because of his friend Kuno, who had recommended his visit.

> They had lived and had gone to school together in an old small city in Texas settled early by the Spaniards. Mexicans, Spaniards, Germans, and Americans mostly from Kentucky had mingled there more or less comfortably for several generations. (*Collected Stories* 437)

The implication is that Charles Upton is somewhat "urbane" and that his disappointment in the Ger-

mans of Berlin is somehow not because of his Texas
upbringing. He has come to Berlin, after all, to become a painter. But he is not prepared for the dreadful conditions in the Berlin of 1931. Kuno, who had
died at the age of fifteen on a visit to Berlin, is ever
on his mind. Significantly, Kuno—like Adam Barclay in "Pale Horse, Pale Rider"—is a "sacrificial"
character; the dead Kuno can now function as a symbol of "the old order" in Germany, an order being
replaced by a colossal war machine. The old Germany is dead; the threatening new Germany is ris-
ing.

Even the weather is threatening to Charles Upton. And the weather reminds him of his Texas origins. "The darkness closed over the strange city like
the great fist of an enemy," he thinks. But he real-
izes that the oppressive weather is partly the prod-
uct of his imagination. He *wants* to hate Berlin, and
the weather provides the necessary excuse:

> At home in Texas he had seen northern trav-
> elers turn upon the southern weather with the
> ferocity of exhaustion; it gave them the excuse
> they needed to hate everything else they hated
> in the place, too.

But Berlin is chiefly hateful, Charles Upton thinks,
because of the piggish faces, piggish notions, pig-
like characteristics of all sorts. The German and the
porcine are synonymous in this tale.

The very atmosphere is animalistic. The weather is "wolfish cold." Snarling cruelty threatens him everywhere he goes. As a foreigner, he is under constant suspicion; and in every way he is exploited by the Germans. Anti-Semitism is rampant. Memories of Kuno, who functions as a metaphor for Texas Germans, intensify Charles Upton's disappointment with the reality of German culture. The Texas Germans, according to Upton's memory, were not at all like the Germans who now mistreat him so casually. Kuno, of German descent, was a gifted violinist; but German art and culture are seen now to be in decay.

When Charles Upton visits a cabaret and gazes at Lutte, an attractive model, doing what was supposed to be a rumba, it seems to Charles more like "a combination of the black bottom and the hoochy-coochy such as he had seen, sneaking off furtively with other boys, in carnival sideshows during his innocent boyhood in Texas." Throughout the story, the implied as well as the explicit contrast is that between Texas and Berlin.

Readers who know Thomas Mann's short story "Mario and the Magician" (1929), a study of Italy's falling under the spell of an oppressive fascism, will recognize a possible influence upon "The Leaning Tower," whose title is suggestive of Italian influences. And one wonders if George Orwell may have in some way been influenced by Porter. His anti-Stalinist fantasy, *Animal Farm*, which was not pub-

lished until 1945, describes a totalitarian state in
which the pigs take charge of the government. But
pigs are, of course, natural symbols of greediness
and unthinking power. Indeed, the police are often
referred to today as "pigs." For Porter, who grew up
in south central Texas, pigs provide a conveniently
ambivalent symbol. Her story "He" is central in this
regard.

For our purposes, "The Leaning Tower" can be
understood as what it felt like to be a Texan in Hitler's Germany in 1931.

V. S. Pritchett, writing in the *New Statesman* (in
an opinion quoted on the book-jacket of *The Leaning
Tower and Other Stories*), praised the story for its
fine technique and its subtle observation:

> Her picture of Berlin in the Isherwood period
> is eerie and searching. She sees everything
> that disturbs. She notices peculiar local things
> that one realises afterwards are true: how of-
> ten, for example, the Berliners' eyes filled with
> tears when they were suddenly faced with
> small dilemmas. Hysteria is near to the sur-
> face. Yet the tears were a kind of mannerism.
> Her power to make a landscape, a room, a
> group of people, thinkingly alive is not the
> vague, brutal talent of the post-Hemingway re-
> porter but belongs to the explicit Jamesian pe-
> riod and suggests the whole rather than the
> surface of a life.

It is indeed the oppressive *atmosphere* that dominates this story, the sense of uneasiness; the fear of
being stopped by the police, of calling attention to
oneself in any way whatsoever; in short, the brutal-
ized, animalized atmosphere of the police state. Not
all critics, it should go without saying, have praised
this work as highly as Pritchett; Ray B. West, for
example, thought that "'The Leaning Tower' comes
the nearest to failure of anything that Katherine
Anne Porter has published" (*KAP* 24). But for most
readers, the atmosphere makes the story, the atmosphere of the German police state. And this is the
picture, for better or worse, that Katherine Anne
Porter consistently paints of Germans and German
culture. And in her only full-length novel, *Ship of
Fools*, it is same song, second verse.

Ship of Fools (1962)

Although a few critics have praised Katherine
Anne Porter's only full-length novel, *Ship of Fools*,
most readers have been disappointed with this work.
The massive number of characters, the needless pro-
liferation of conversations, the unsavory theme, the
unsatisfactory closure, the patent anti-German ideology, and the tendency to complicate what ought to
be simple plot structure—all this puts the reader off.
As Texans might say, "that dog won't hunt."

Mark Schorer, reviewing the book for the *New*

York Times on April 1, 1962, praised the work lav-
ishly, ranking it as one of the greatest novels of the
century. And M. M. Liberman, in a series of critical
articles, has consistently defended *Ship of Fools* as a
great novel.

But others have disliked the work intensely. Chief
among the faults obvious to every reader is the extreme repetitiveness caused by Porter's method of
repeating conversations, already known to the
reader in one connection, on other separate occasions with other characters. Stagnation, lack of
movement, absence of growth and change are noted
by critics as well.

There is a critical danger lurking here. Scholars
and critics of Porter's work—knowledgeable in the
details of her wanderings, associates, varied experiences, and attitudes—display a tendency to overrate
Ship of Fools because, *to them*, the work is of considerable interest. It must be remembered, at the
same time, that the general public has not devoted
its waking life to the details of Katherine Anne Porter's biography; for the vast majority of readers,
Ship of Fools is an artistic failure.

James Ward Lee's *Classics of Texas Fiction* (1987)
does not list Porter's *Ship of Fools* anywhere among
the forty-seven novels by thirty-eight Texas novel-
ists reviewed for his influential guide to Texas fiction.

Porter was not, as some have thought, without experience in the writing of novels. She had actually ghost-written a lengthy novel, *My Chinese Marriage*, published in 1921 (Givner *KAP* 149–50, 526). And in 1942 she had published a translation from the Spanish (actually a complete rewriting in English) of José Joaquín Fernandez de Lizárdi's novel, *El Perequillo Sarniento*, published as *The Itching Parrot* (Givner *KAP* 340). And she had, of course, written short novels, or novellas, with great distinction.

The setting of the novel owes most to Porter's 1931 voyage (along with her companion, Eugene Pressly) aboard the German ship SS *Werra* from Veracruz, Mexico, to Bremerhaven, Germany, as well as the five months spent in Berlin in that same year. In addition, the voyage taken by Porter and Pressly in 1936 on their return from Europe to New York comes into play. The stormy relationship between Jenny Brown and David Scott is, of course, based upon these and other experiences of Porter and Pressly (Givner *KAP* 298).

As Porter informs the reader in her brief preface, "the title of this book is a translation from the German of *Das Narrenschiff*, a moral allegory by Sebastian Brant." The implication is that *Ship of Fools* is to be some sort of complex moral allegory. Such is not the case. *Ship of Fools* must be judged as what it is—a realistic novel in the tradition of the comedy of manners. And as such, it cannot be said to rank high in the world's literature.

Ship of Fools is conceived on a grand scale, worthy of a Texas circus barker. Numerous characters, interacting in a multiplicity of ways, discussing many situations from pluralistic sets of assumptions, reveal to the reader much more than he probably is interested in knowing about all these things. Most of the passengers are Germans returning to Germany from Mexico at just the moment in history (the reader knows this from hindsight) when they ought not to be going anywhere near Germany. The gross Rieber, publisher of a magazine dealing with women's clothes, has dishonorable intentions toward the dizzy-headed Lizzi. The childless couple, Professor and Frau Hutten, treat their seasick white bulldog Bébé with sickening sentimentality. Baumgartner, failed attorney and hopeless alcoholic, has nothing to look forward to. Karl Glocken, a miserable hunchback, has sold out his little tobacco and newspaper stand in Mexico and aims, without much expectation, to begin anew in Germany. Graf, a religious enthusiast, is dying of an incurable illness, but believes, in his deliriums, that God has given him the power of healing others. A corrupt, money-grabbing, zarzuela company of Spanish dancers scheme to defraud the other passengers of their money. And there are four Americans: William Denny, a Texas chemical engineer on his way to Berlin; Mary Tread-well, a woman of forty-five and divorced; David Scott and Jenny Brown, two young painters living to-gether who torment and love one another in turn. Down in the steerage are more than eight hundred migrant workers, being deported to Spain after the failure of the sugar market in Cuba; their "La Condessa," a drug addict, can offer them little reas-surance.

The story is fashioned by the depiction of the in-termingling and intercommunication of all these various characters. They are all "fools" because they are blind to the disaster that awaits them (the rise of Hitler, World War II, and the holocaust). In episodes portraying personal unkindness, cruelty, stubborn prejudice, hatred, and bigotry, Porter shows that all the characters are devoid of genuine love, lacking substantial hope for the future, and even incapable of meaningful action.

Ship of Fools contains some mighty and memora-ble passages, but it fails to maintain, as a novel, the interest of the reader. Were it not such a cliché, one might at this point recall Gertrude Stein's remark about the literary works of Thomas Wolfe, the quip about "moments of greatness and hours of some-thing altogether different."

The novel is divided into three parts, each with its

supposedly appropriate epigraph. Part I, "Embarkation," is ostensibly intended to be emblematic of Baudelaire's question, "When will we embark in the direction of happiness?" This section deals, as one would expect, with the preparations for the journey, the preliminaries in Veracruz, and the introduction of some of the characters. Part II, "High Sea," takes its epigraph from Brahms's song title, "Keine Haus, Keine Heimat" (Without home, without homeland) and deals with the events on board ship while it is on the high seas. Part III, "The Harbors" has as its epigraph a quotation from Saint Paul, "For here have we no continuing city." Thus the three stages of the ship's voyage account for the three parts of the novel. Those who have seen the three divisions of the novel as in any way allegorical or symbolic have not been convincing in their arguments.

The themes of *Ship of Fools* are summarized in a straightforward manner by Darlene Unrue as follows:

> The illusions which people create and live by are explored in particular ways, but the grand illusion that guides the ship is that they are all going forward to something better. The reality is that they are going forward to something worse than their wildest imaginings. In this pell-mell race to the future, the voyagers are isolated from one another in, for the most part,

loveless existences. They mistake or substitute
lust, orderliness, or zeal for love, which Porter
shows to be the mystery of life capable of unit-
ing all people. She also takes up the question of
evil, its sources and its nourishment in contemporary society. (*Understanding KAP* 125–26)

Furthermore, says Unrue, although the characters
"are being carried by 'truth' (the *Vera*)," they are too
blind to understand it. What is missing is the "allegory" that the reader has been promised by the author in the brief preface, the allegory of "the ship of
this world on its voyage to eternity." Besides, Porter
is completely occupied in this novel with characterization, and this preoccupation gets in the way of
thematic development.

Overemphasis upon characterization is, in fact,
the cause of the artistic failure of the novel. The
reader cannot digest and assimilate all the information that Porter provides about an excessive number
of characters. The very fact that the author felt it
necessary to provide a list of "Characters" at the
beginning of the novel is ominous. The vast array of
characters are classified as German, Swiss, Spanish,
Cuban, Mexican, Swedish, American, those "in
steerage," and cabin mates. The total number of
characters that Porter individualizes with names
and particular histories is forty-one. But there are
numerous characters (even animals) that are talked

about in the course of the voyage. There are frequent
allusions to the eight hundred and seventy-six souls
"in steerage," but there is little individuation of
these. The reader must frequently refer to this pas-
senger list in order to follow the conversations that
go on interminably aboard ship. And those characters that we *do* get to know, we get to know *too well*.
Stanley Kauffmann, reviewing the novel for the
New Republic, wrote that "The characters are well
perceived and described, but we know all that Miss
Porter can say about them after the third or fourth
of their episodes" (24).

It is the "Texas" character that particularly interests us here. As A. C. Greene has observed, Texas
writers seem to have some sort of obsession with
Texas stereotypes. "The myth," he says, "won't let
Texas inspect itself with reality. It is impossible to
write a novel about Texas using only so-called ordinary people. A 'Texas character' must be included"
(Clifford 46). And Katherine Anne Porter certainly
did not escape the Texas mythology when she wrote
Ship of Fools. While *Ship of Fools* is more than a
"novel about Texas," it does indeed include its
"Texas character," one of the four Americans aboard
the Vera. And the character, it turns out, is a com-
posite of some of the worst character traits ever visited upon a hapless literary character. Joan Givner
quotes Porter's letter to Caroline Gordon, dated 28

August 1931, from aboard the SS *Werra*, concerning
a young Texas oculist on board ship. Porter was contemplating the swirling mass of humanity in the
steerage section of the ship when her thoughts were
interrupted:

> As a young oculist from Texas, on his way to
> Vienna for a special clinic of some kind, com-
> mented: "It isn't as if they were dirty Bolshe-
> viks." I was so startled by this remark, as a
> voice from the prehistoric times of the world,
> that I asked involuntarily, "Where are you
> from?" It seemed, Austin, Houston, Corpus
> Christi, Texas. Still, so help me, they are talk-
> ing that way in Texas. . . . He represents a
> great part of whatever enlightenment that
> place has to offer. (*KAP* 249)

William Denny, the unpleasant Texan of *Ship of
Fools*, is based in part on this young Texas oculist.
But, as Givner also believes, Porter's first husband,
John Henry Koontz of Inez, Texas, also—in her own
mind—an unpleasant Texan, was partially the
model for William Denny; indeed, Porter had already, in "Holiday" (1960), displaced East Texas
Swiss as "Germans" in her story dealing with relatives of her first husband.

William Denny, the "tall shambling young Texan," who refers to the Cuban female entertainers as

"Chili Queens," and calls the clerk at the Immigrations Office "Pancho," is a native of Brownsville, Texas, a town that he prefers above all others because in that place, "a man knew who was who and who was what, and niggers, crazy Swedes, Jews, greasers, boneheaded Micks, polacks, wops, Guineas and damn Yankees knew their place and stayed in it" (24). His racism and intolerance are obvious. But he is only one example among many characters guilty of the most vicious bigotry. As the novel progresses, Denny shows how he is absolutely without redeeming social value. He goes through the novel lusting after women, boozing at all hours, insulting the other passengers, and in general making a fool out of himself, just as a caricature of the boorish Texan (which is exactly what he is), is supposed to do. In a moment of frustration over his lack of success with the prostitutes, Denny remarks to David Scott, "Women peddling tail don't usually carry it so high, where I come from. It's just cash on the barrelhead and no hurt feelings" (52). Speaking of the unfortunates in the steerage section of the ship, he observes, "Poor devils, they don't deserve it . . . They're not dirty Reds, the papers said so" (60). Encountering Mrs. Treadwell for the first time, "His gaze ran like a hand to her ears, her neck, over her breasts, down her thighs, and his mouth was bitter as if he did not like what he saw, but could not control the roving of his eyes" (61). Lusting after Pastora, he curses the difficulty of finding her alone, thinking that he can succeed (even with the pittance he is willing to pay), "if I can ever get her cut out from the herd" (78). He knows that he is lowering his standards when he chases a Cuban female, saying "Up to now I've never had anything to do with anybody but white girls" (280). His general attitude towards women is illustrated in his advice to David Scott on how to control his girlfriend, Jenny: "I never mix in anybody's business, understand, but if that bitch belonged to me, I'd break every bone in her" (438). When David Scott tries to inform him that he is a painter, Denny thinks, predictably, that Scott means that he paints houses and signboards (75). Speaking to Herr Lowenthal, the Jew who sells plastic rosaries and wooden saint statues, and thinking to insult him, Denny blurts: "If there's one religion on this earth that I despise, it's those Catholics. I don't like anything about 'em. Where I come from, only the lowest kind of people, greasers and wops and polacks, are Catholics, and I say they can have it—it's good enough for 'em" (96). But he is more tolerant on the subject of Jews: "We didn't have a thing against Jews in our town—we didn't even have any Jews!" (275). His drinking is systematic; "I aim to be stinkin' before this here night is done," (127) is his usual announcement. But, needless to say, his taste in alcohol is basic: "Denny . . . thought champagne, even the best, tasted like thin vinegar with bubbles in it" (278).

When Denny, in a drunken rage, crashes into Mrs. Treadwell's cabin, mistaking it for that of Pastora, he is quickly on the receiving end of an overly severe beating:

> Mrs. Treadwell doubled her fist and struck him sharply, again and again, in the mouth, on the cheek, on the nose. The blows hurt her hand and seemed to make no impression on Denny. He moved as if he might get up. Feeling her sandal under her, she took it off and held it firmly by the sole and beat him in the face and head with the heel, breathlessly, rising on her knees and coming nearer, her lips drawn back and her teeth set. She beat him with such furious pleasure a sharp pain started up in her right wrist and shot to her shoulder and neck. The sharp metal-capped high heels at every blow broke the skin in small half moons that slowly turned scarlet, and as they multiplied on his forehead, cheeks, chin, lips, Mrs. Treadwell grew cold with fright at what she was doing, yet could not for her life stop herself. (465–65)

Not since "A Days's Work" (1940) had Katherine Anne Porter indulged herself by depicting such a brutal attack upon a hated symbol of masculine grossness. The drunken Denny represents to her, at this moment in the novel, all that she most wants to lash out against. But even in the alter-ego of Mrs. Treadwell, the justification for the extremity of the beating seems lacking. Overkill is the name of Mrs. Treadwell's (and Katherine Anne Porter's) game. Denny certainly asked for it. But there are limits, one would think, to revenge. The stereotypical Texan must be beaten out of Porter's system.

Texas, in the William Denny incarnation, does not come off shiningly.

From an autobiographical standpoint, Katherine Anne Porter seems to have split herself into two parts in *Ship of Fools*. Jenny Brown, the aspiring painter, who is living and traveling with David Scott (whose painting and spiritual deadness she cannot respect even though she loves him in her own way) represents that side of Porter that one may call the Miranda/Laura portrait. She struggles to make sense of life around her. She is young, beautiful, and eager for life, whatever may come of it. The other side of Katherine Anne Porter, Mrs. Treadwell, "a woman of forty-five, divorced, returning to Paris," is the character closest to Katherine Anne Porter at the time of publication of *Ship of Fools*. In Mrs. Treadwell, Porter engages in a great deal of self-examination. Her observations, though ironically

humorous in tone, require special attention. But
Mrs. Treadwell is really a caricature of the "genteel"
lady, afraid of life, of risk, of any commitment whatever. Her future does not seem rosy. She is not in
any sense a feminist (that typical Porterian function
being left in this novel to the ambivalent Frau Hutten, wife of Professor Hutten). Fittingly, it is the
"genteel" Mrs. Treadwell who will avenge herself
upon the coarse Texan, William Denny. And, for
most Texas readers, it couldn't happen to a nicer
fellow.

Just as the Grandmother in Porter's early Texas
fiction is a metaphor for Texas, or for the South in
Texas civilization, so William Denny is clearly the
metaphor for Texas in *Ship of Fools*. All readers of
Ship of Fools have gasped upon reading the account
of Mrs. Treadwell's rather brutal beating of the
drunken Denny, a beating that involves far greater
violence than is strictly necessary to quell his mistaken advances, and a violent act performed upon an
individual helpless to defend himself while in a
drunken stupor. No doubt, such scenes helped Porter
to psychological revenge upon the gross or ineffectual males of the world who (like her Texas father)
unwittingly caused great human suffering for all
those connected with them. The clinical perspective
in the Treadwell/Denny scene certainly does remind
us of that same quality in "A Day's Work." It is
probably true also, as George Hendrick and others

believe, that the drunken outrages of Hart Crane, who had visited her in Mexico some years earlier, contributed a part to the characterization of William Denny. Crane's excessive drinking and obscene outbursts were extremely distressing to Porter, just as William Denny's crude behavior is so shocking and repulsive to Mrs. Treadwell (a lady not completely unlike Katherine Anne Porter).

The Mexican elements in the novel will be of interest to all who followed Porter's literary career. Mexico, with its seemingly insoluble social problems, the betrayal inherent in the Revolution of 1910, and the generally arrogant and unpleasant attitudes of foreigners in its midst, is not a new theme in Porter work. Porter's readers could not help but recall the 1934 story "Hacienda" as a possible genesis for *Ship of Fools*.

Readers of "The Leaning Tower" (1941) and "Holiday" (1960) had noted the excessive disgust which Porter had lavished upon what she considered piggish Germans. Her distaste for Germans and German culture amount to overkill in *Ship of Fools*. Maurice Kasten writes:

> Miss Porter's Germans are gross, sensual, sentimental paranoiacs bravest and most comfortable when running in a pack. Usually they are described with palpable malice, and when there is a rare note of compassion, it is offered

without respect . . . a note of irony and contempt is always present. (55)

And John Thompson writes,

All the characters are hateful and it is a
pleasure to see each in turn get his lumps.
Most of them are piggish Germans. They suffer
for it. (611)

Most readers readily agree. Yet the Jews, the victims of the Germans, do not come off any better;
still, it seems misleading to call Katherine Anne
Porter anti-Semitic; the Jews seem no more despicable, and certainly not any better, than all the
other miserable characters aboard the Vera.

In terms of plot, there is nothing but talk, talk,
talk. The reader yearns for a bit of adventure, a
yearning that is never satisfied. John Thompson,
noting that a novel set on a ship at sea deserves at
least some of the conventional devices to excite a
reader, observes,

There is no plot . . . no sea adventures, no
hurricanes or mutinies, only a dog overboard.
Instead of a plot, there is a complex mounting
of tensions and forced or sought intimacies of
the passengers. (611)

Indeed, when would there be time to depict such
conventional or exciting incidents? The characters

must be attended to! And the massive number of characters to contend with mitigates against any meaningful plot. As William Abrahams has observed,

> While there is enormous consistency of the characterization, there is remarkably little plot development. Miss Porter's interest is elsewhere: she gains an effect of progression through endless repetition. (808)

"Endless repetition" is precisely the effect the unfortunate reader experiences; moreover, it is repetition that seems to go nowhere. Indeed, who can honestly deny the truth of Smith Kirkpatrick's view that "the novel comes to no conclusions, answers no questions; its ending is the end of the journey" (98)?

Even though *Ship of Fools* must be regarded as an artistic failure, it is fortunate that we have it. The novel is valuable, if for no other reason, because it offers assistance in the interpretation of Porter's short fiction. Just as Melville's *Pierre* offers clues to the proper understanding of *Moby-Dick*, so *Ship of Fools* provides an index to clearer understanding of Katherine Anne Porter's short stories. And the novel *does* contain some passages of magnificent writing, not the least of which is the devastating caricature of William Denny, citizen of Brownsville, Texas.

For Texans, bigger is better. Katherine Anne Porter had been goaded into writing a full-length novel. While this was an artistic mistake, it at least enabled her to profit financially from a lifetime of dedicated effort in her craft. And the commercially successful motion picture adapted from the novel did a world of good for her literary reputation. Surely, she realized that she was essentially a miniaturist, a genius in the genre of the short story. It was the mistaken critical notions of novel lovers that caused her to undertake and finally finish a full-length novel. *Ship of Fools* did nothing for her reputation. But neither did it do any harm to her reputation as the greatest of the short story writers of her generation. And it will continue to be of interest to Porter scholars and critics who seek to clarify relationships between her troubled life and her creative works.

7

CONCLUSION

Craig Clifford speaks of "the tension between the power of place and the denial of place which the life of the intellect tends to create" ("Horseman, Hang On" 51). No writer illustrates the principle better than Katherine Anne Porter. She found it necessary to deny her origins in order to compete in what seemed to her a larger world; ironically, it was the place of her birth and upbringing that contributed most to her success in that other world. What Clifford terms "the overpowering presence of the rural tradition in Texas culture" is indeed reflected in Porter's work, though it is sometimes its *denial* that is most significant in her case.

Katherine Anne Porter never forgot her roots. Circumstances and opportunities led her to leave Texas and remain outside Texas for many years, but she remained throughout her lifetime a Texas writer nonetheless. Two great disappointments caused Katherine Anne Porter to doubt the affection of Texans for herself and for her literary work. First, the

1939 decision of the Texas Institute of Letters to
deny her its prize (for *Pale Horse, Pale Rider*) for the
best work of fiction to appear during that year came
as a great shock to her. When J. Frank Dobie was
given the award instead (for *Apache Gold and Yaqui
Silver*), and when the rationale for the awarding of
the prize was so obscurely stated, she was thoroughly disgusted. Second, in 1958, when the ru-
mored naming of a library in her honor at the University of Texas did not materialize, she determined
to leave her papers to another library. It is still not
certain just how far the University of Texas had
planned to go in this affair; nevertheless, in Porter's
mind, this was another Texas insult to a Texas girl.
There were numerous other "slights" of this kind
that saddened Katherine Anne Porter.

A partial reconciliation was effected in Katherine
Anne Porter's eighty-sixth year when she was invited to accept an honorary degree from Howard
Payne University, an obscure denominational
school located near her childhood haunts. It was during this visit that she decided to have her remains
brought back to Indian Creek to lie beside those of
her mother. She came to feel that old grievances
should be laid aside. But her literary remains are
not housed in Texas; they reside at the McKeldin
Library at the University of Maryland. As Joan
Givner has so aptly noted, "This two-fold disposition

of her remains correctly indicates that the ambivalences of a lifetime were never finally resolved" ("Katherine Anne Porter and the Southwest" 559).

Porter's extreme sensitivity to adverse criticism and her yearning for critical approval caused her to develop antipathies and friendships that were sometimes unwise. Her lashing out at critics that supposedly did not understand her work did little to enhance her reputation. Her feminine "bitchiness" was duly noted in an age that condoned Hemingway's tough-guy antics.

Katherine Anne Porter was not highly educated, in a formal sense. But she read widely and creatively. Perhaps because of a slight inferiority complex, she fitted herself into the "self-made" mold of the Texas tradition. There was, indeed, something of the Texas con artist in her. Her numerous misleading interviews helped her create just the right image to keep her work before the public eye, and her humor—both in her fiction and in her resplendent conversation—reminds us of the southwestern tradition of the tall tale.

Porter's position in Texas letters remains a troubled one. Too often, she is simply dismissed as "Texas's greatest writer," and then casually tossed over as one who did not want to be associated with Texas. Nevertheless most Texas critics rank her work very high indeed. The publication of Joan Givner's biog-

raphy *Katherine Anne Porter: A Life* in 1982 has
done wonders for her reputation in Texas; for it demonstrates the close ties that Porter always maintained with her native state and with friends there.
But as the first Texan to achieve truly national (and
even international) stature in literature, Katherine
Anne Porter cannot be dismissed from any historical
or critical account of Texas literature. As an "expatriate" Porter must take her lumps; but so do Henry
James, T. S. Eliot, James Joyce, and many others.
Yet it *does* seem quite old fashioned to attack expatriates as somehow lacking in regional loyalty just
because they have not remained in close geographical proximity to their native lands. In imagination,
all the above named expatriates were true to their
homelands.

Katherine Anne Porter's subject matter was what
could have been expected of a Texas writer of her
generation. Edmund Wilson has classified her stories into three categories: family life, pictures of foreign parts, and stories about women; all are related
to her Texas upbringing. Considerable misreading
has no doubt gone on, especially in Porter's stories of
the old South. A re-reading of these stories shows
convincingly that Old South stereotypes were indeed *rejected* by her, not furthered in her literary
art.

Porter's stories with Texas settings demonstrate

her love for her native state, albeit her love is intermixed with large doses of distaste for the stifling of
individuality and creativity inherent in the social
context of her upbringing. She never forgot the very
difficult and impoverished childhood she had under-
gone in Texas. And the father that she judged to be
ineffectual, lazy, and incompetent for large affairs
was to be the model for many such males in her
fiction. The exasperation, voiced by her ironic narrators, expressed at the expense of ineffectual males
without gumption, is one of the hallmarks of her
fiction.

Porter's feminism, in fact, stems from her impres-
sions of her Texas father's inadequacies and her
Texas grandmother's surpassing competence. Further, Porter's descriptions of marriage are closely
related to her memories of her childhood in Texas.
Marriage is seldom or never idyllically presented in
her fiction, and males are seldom sufficient for the
task at hand. Over and over again, this situation
occurs in her fiction. Porter's most important characters are women whose preoccupations are symp-
tomatic of the condition of modern womanhood.
Jane DeMouy, in *Katherine Anne Porter's Women:
The Eye of Her Fiction* (1983) calls the Porter canon
"a sensitive prophecy for contemporary femininity"
(13).

Even in stories without a specifically Texas setting, Katherine Anne Porter was essentially a Texas writer. *Pale Horse, Pale Rider*, for instance, is set in Denver, Colorado; but its Texas-born hero, who must die in order for the plot to fulfill itself, is evidence of Porter's troubled relationship with her home state. And in "The Cracked Looking-Glass," ostensibly set in Connecticut, Porter summons up her rural experiences of fundamentalist Christianity in a surprising context. And in "The Leaning Tower," it is *the Texan*, Charles Upton, who deals with the Berlin of 1931 in a way that only a Texan could. Numerous examples of the effects of Porter's Texas upbringing occur throughout her fiction, regardless of the fictional setting.

Porter's Mexican stories, as well as those stories dealing with other areas of the United States and with foreign countries, show how she was able to transplant the experiences of her Texas childhood onto narratives ostensibly dealing with alien parts. One can note, to take just one example, the protagonist of "That Tree," set in Mexico, who is clearly based on Porter's Texas father.

Katherine Anne Porter was not primarily interested in social reform; she was, rather, a *reporter* of the social scene. She profoundly disliked propagandistic or overtly didactic art. And her highly developed sense of humor (a subject that awaits extensive scholarly study) was not employed to subvert the social order; rather, her humor slyly *comments* on the status quo. Had she written several full-length novels, she would have been the Jane Austen of our literature; she is, rather, the De Maupassant of American literature, supreme in the field of the short story, with the stories that sport a Texas scenery the very greatest. She is a link in the great realistic tradition of Austen and James, infatuated with the comedy of manners, the moral basis of human relationships. Givner reports that one of Katherine Anne Porter's favorite axioms, to which she never found a single exception, was "There is no such thing as an exact synonym and no such thing as an unmixed motive" (*KAP* 386). And it was her Texas upbringing that contributed most to her understanding of ambivalent motivations and unique expression. She herself never really forgot that. This "refugee from Indian Creek," as Hank Lopez called her, remained true to her roots.

Katherine Anne Porter's literary style owed most to her Texas upbringing. As Joan Givner notes,

> she forged out of the soft rhythms of southern speech and the racy idioms of her native Texas a unique style, at once elegant and tough, lyrical and vigorous, formal and witty, truly a classical style for all occasions. (511)

Most noticeably, of course, her mastery of this style occurs in regional dialogue.

More revealing than anything else in the troubled relationship between Katherine Anne Porter and Texas is that, at the last, she chose to be buried beside her mother in the little cemetery at Indian Creek, Texas.

SELECTED BIBLIOGRAPHY

PRIMARY SOURCES

WORKS BY KATHERINE ANNE PORTER

A Christmas Story. New York: Seymour Lawrence, 1967.

The Collected Essays and Occasional Writings of Katherine Anne Porter. New York: Delacorte Press, 1970. Rpt. New York: Dell, 1973; Boston: Houghton Mifflin/Seymour Lawrence, 1990.

The Collected Stories of Katherine Anne Porter. New York: Harcourt, Brace & World, 1965. Rpt. New York: New American Library, 1970. Includes the stories previously published in *Flowering Judas and Other Stories* (1930); *Pale Horse, Pale Rider* (1939), a collection of three short novels: "Pale Horse, Pale Rider," "Old Mortality," and "Noon Wine"; and *The Leaning Tower and Other Stories* (1944); in addition, the previously uncollected stories, "The Martyr," "Virgin Violeta," "The Fig Tree," and "Holiday" are included. "The Old Order" (from *The Leaning Tower and Other Stories*) is here re-titled "The Journey."

The Days Before. New York: Harcourt, Brace, 1952. Critical and miscellaneous essays.

The Itching Parrot. Translation by Porter, from the Spanish, of José Joaquín Fernandez de Lizárdi's *El Perequillo Sarniento*. Garden City: Doubleday, 1942. This work is actually a complete rewriting in English of the Spanish novel.

Katherine Anne Porter: Conversations. Ed. Joan Givner. Jackson: UP of Mississippi, 1987.

Katherine Anne Porter's French Song Book. Paris: Harrison, 1933.

Letters of Katherine Anne Porter. Ed. Isabel Bayley. Boston: Atlantic Monthly Press, 1990.

My Chinese Marriage (signed "M. T. F."). New York: Duffield, 1921. A novel completely ghost-written by Porter.

The Never-Ending Wrong. Boston: Little, Brown & Co., 1977. "Notes on the Texas I Remember." *The Atlantic* (March 1975): 102- 06. This essay is not included in *The Collected Essays and Occasional Writings of Katherine Anne Porter*.

Outline of Mexican Popular Arts and Crafts. Los Angeles: Young and McCallister, 1922.

Ship of Fools. Boston: Atlantic-Little, Brown & Co., 1962; Rpt. New York: New American Library, 1963.

What Price Marriage? New York: J. H. Sears, 1927. Compiled, edited, and with an Introduction by Porter (under pseudonym "Hamblen Sears") .

BIBLIOGRAPHICAL GUIDES

Bixby, George. "Katherine Anne Porter: A Bibliographical Checklist." *American Book Collector* 1 (1980): 19– 33.

Ebeling-Koning, Blanche T., Curator. "The Katherine Anne Porter Collection: 94 MS. Boxes." College Park, MD: University of Maryland Libraries, 1978. Accession number 105. Mimeographed.

Givner, Joan, Jane DeMouy, and Ruth M. Alvarez. "Katherine Anne Porter." In *American Women Writers: A Critical Reference Guide from Colonial Times to the Present*, ed. Lina Mainiero. New York: Ungar, 1979. 201–31.

Hendrick, Willene, and George Hendrick. "Selected Bibliography." In *Katherine Anne Porter: Revised Edition*. Boston: Twayne, 1988. 149–57.

Hilt, Kathryn. *Katherine Anne Porter: A Bibliography*. New York: Garland, 1985.

Kiernan, Robert F. *Katherine Anne Porter and Carson McCullers: A Reference Guide*. Boston: G. K. Hall, 1976.

Lopez, Enrique Hank. "Selected Bibliography." In *Conversations with Katherine Anne Porter: Refugee from Indian Creek*. Boston: Little, Brown, and Co., 1981. 311–15.

Schwartz, Edward. "Katherine Anne Porter: A Critical Bibliography." *Bulletin of the New York Public Library* 57 (1953): 211–47. Rpt. *Katherine Anne Porter: A Critical Bibliography*. Folcroft, PA: Folcroft Press, 1969.

Unrue, Darlene Harbour. "Bibliography." In *Understanding Katherine Anne Porter*. Columbia, SC: U of South Carolina Press, 1988. 171–85.

Wade, Sally Dee. "A Texas Bibliography of Katherine Anne Porter." In *Katherine Anne Porter and Texas: An Uneasy Relationship*. Ed. Clinton Machann and William Bedford Clark. Boston: Atlantic Monthly Press, 1990. 124–82.

Waldrip, Louise, and Shirley Ann Bauer. *A Bibliography of the Works of Katherine Anne Porter and A Bibliography of the Criticism of the Works of Katherine Anne Porter*. Metuchen, NJ: Scarecrow Press, 1969.

GENERAL SCHOLARSHIP ON PORTER'S LIFE AND WORKS

Aldridge, John W. "Art and Passion in Katherine Anne Porter." In *Katherine Anne Porter: A Critical Symposium*, ed. Lodwick Hartley and George Core. Athens: U of Georgia P, 1969. 97–102.

Allen, Charles A. "Katherine Anne Porter: Psychology As Art." *Southwest Review* 41 (1956): 223–30.

—. "The Nouvelles of Katherine Anne Porter." *University of Kansas City Review* 29 (1962): 87–93.

—. "Southwestern Chronicle: Katherine Anne Porter." *Arizona Quarterly* 2 (1946): 90–95.

Baumgartner, Paul R. *Katherine Anne Porter*. New York: American Authors and Critics Series, 1969.

Bloom, Harold, ed. *Katherine Anne Porter*. Edited with an introduction by Harold Bloom. Modern Critical Views. New York: Chelsea House, 1986.

Bode, Winston. "Miss Porter on Writers and Writing." *Texas Observer* 31 October 1958: 6–7.

Booth, Wayne C. *The Rhetoric of Fiction.* 2nd ed. Chicago: U of Chicago P, 1983. 61–62, 274–77, *passim.*

Bride, Sister Mary, O.P. "Laura and the Unlit Lamp." *Studies in Short Fiction* 1 (1963): 61–63.

Brinkmeyer, Robert H., Jr. "'Endless Remembering': The Artistic Vision of Katherine Anne Porter." *Mississippi Quarterly* 40 (Winter 1986–87): 5–19.

Brooks, Cleanth. *A Shaping Joy: Studies in the Writer's Craft.* New York: Harcourt, Brace, 1971. *passim.* See especially the chapter entitled "The Southern Temper."

Core, George. "The Best Residuum of Truth." *Georgia Review* 20 (1966): 278–91.

DeMouy, Jane Krause. *Katherine Anne Porter's Women: The Eye of Her Fiction.* Austin: U of Texas P, 1983.

Emmons, Winfred S. *Katherine Anne Porter: The Regional Stories.* Southwest Writers Series, no. 6. Austin: Steck-Vaughn, 1967.

Flanders, Jane. "Katherine Anne Porter and the Ordeal of Southern Womanhood." *Southern Literary Journal* 9 (1976): 47–60.

—. "Katherine Anne Porter's Feminist Criticism: Book Reviews from the 1920's." *Frontiers: A Journal of Women's Studies* 2 (1979): 44–48.

Gaston, Edwin W., Jr. "The Mythic South of Katherine Anne Porter." *Southwestern American Literature* 3 (1973): 81–85.

Givner, Joan. *Katherine Anne Porter: A Life.* New York: Simon & Schuster, 1982. The definitive biography.

—. "Katherine Anne Porter and the Southwest." In *A Literary History of the American West*. Sponsored by The Western Literature Association. J. Golden Taylor, Editor-in-Chief. Fort Worth: Texas Christian UP, 1987. 559–66.

—. "Katherine Anne Porter, Journalist." In *Katherine Anne Porter*. Edited with an introduction by Harold Bloom. Modern Critical Views. New York: Chelsea House, 1986. 69–80. Originally appeared in *Southwest Review* in 1979.

—. "Katherine Anne Porter: The Old Order and the New." In *The Texas Literary Tradition*, ed. Don Graham, James W. Lee, and William T. Pilkington. Austin: U of Texas, 1983. 58–68.

—. "'The Plantation of this Isle': Katherine Anne Porter's Bermuda Base." *Southwest Review* 62 (1978): 339–51.

Gordon, Caroline. "Katherine Anne Porter and the ICM." *Harper's* (November 1964): 146–48.

Gretlund, Jan Nordby. "Katherine Anne Porter and the South: A Corrective." *Mississippi Quarterly* 34 (1981): 435–45.

Gunn, Drewey Wayne. "'Second Country': Katherine Anne Porter." *American and British Writers in Mexico, 1556–1973*. Austin: U of Texas P, 1969.

Hardy, John Edward. *Katherine Anne Porter*. Modern Literature Monographs. New York: Ungar, 1973.

Hartley, Lodwick, and George Core, eds. *Katherine Anne Porter: A Critical Symposium*. Athens: U of Georgia P, 1969.

Hendrick, George. Review of Joan Givner, *Katherine Anne Porter: A Life*. *Texas Books in Review* 5 (1983): 3–4.

Hendrick, Willene, and George Hendrick. *Katherine Anne Porter: Revised Edition*. Boston: Twayne, 1988. George Hendrick's *Katherine Anne Porter* was originally published by Twayne in 1965.

Hennessy, Rosemary. "Katherine Anne Porter's Model for Heroines." *Colorado Quarterly* 25 (1977): 301–15.

Johnson, James William. "Another Look at Katherine Anne Porter." *Virginia Quarterly Review* 36 (1960): 598–613.

Johnson, Shirley E. "Love Attitudes in the Fiction of Katherine Anne Porter." *West Virginia University Philological Papers* 13 (1961): 82–93.

Jones, Anne Goodwyn. "Gender and the Great War: The Case of Faulkner and Porter." *Women's Studies* 13 (1986): 135–48.

Joselyn, Sister M. "Animal Imagery in Katherine Anne Porter's Fiction." In *Myth and Symbol: Critical Approaches and Applications*, ed. Bernice Slote. Lincoln: U of Nebraska P, 1963. 101–15.

Kaplan, Charles. "True Witness: Katherine Anne Porter." *Colorado Quarterly* 7 (1959): 319–27.

Krishnamurthi, M. G. *Katherine Anne Porter: A Study*. Mysore, India: Rao and Raghaven, 1971.

Liberman, M. M. *Katherine Anne Porter's Fiction*. Detroit: Wayne State UP, 1971.

—. "Meeting Miss Porter." *Georgia Review* 41 (1987): 299–303.

Lopez, Enrique Hank. *Conversations with Katherine Anne Porter: Refugee from Indian Creek*. Boston: Little, Brown and Co., 1981.

Machann, Clinton, and William Bedford Clark, eds. *Katherine Anne Porter and Texas: An Uneasy Relationship*. College Station: Texas A&M UP, 1990.

Marsden, M. M. "Love as a Threat in Katherine Anne Porter's Fiction." *Twentieth Century Literature* 13 (1967): 29–38.

Mooney, Harry John, Jr. *The Fiction and Criticism of Katherine Anne Porter*. Critical Essays in Modern Literature series. Rev. ed. Pittsburgh: U of Pittsburgh P, 1962.

Nance, William L. "Katherine Anne Porter and Mexico." *Southwest Review* 55 (Spring 1970): 143–53.

—. *Katherine Anne Porter and the Art of Rejection*. Chapel Hill: U of North Carolina P, 1964.

Partridge, Colin. "'My Familiar Country': An Image of Mexico in the Work of Katherine Anne Porter." *Studies in Short Fiction* 7 (1970): 597–614.

Poss, S. H. "Variations on a Theme in Four Stories of Katherine Anne Porter." *Twentieth Century Literature* 4 (1958): 21–29.
    The four stories are "The Circus," "Old Mortality," "Pale Horse, Pale Rider," and "The Grave."

Ryan, Marjorie. "*Dubliners* and the Stories of Katherine Anne Porter." *American Literature* 31 (1960): 464–73.

Schwartz, Edward Greenfield. "The Fiction of Memory." *Southwest Review* 45 (1960): 204–15.

—. "The Way of Dissent: Katherine Anne Porter's Critical Position." *Western Humanities Review* 8 (1954): 119–30.

Unrue, Darlene H. *Truth and Vision in Katherine Anne Porter's Fiction*. Athens: U of Georgia P, 1985.

—. *Understanding Katherine Anne Porter*. Columbia: U of South Carolina P, 1988.

Vliet, R. G. "On a Literature of the Southwest: An Address." *Texas Observer* (28 April 1978): 18.

Voss, Arthur. "Symbolism and Sensibility: Katherine Anne Porter." In *The American Short Story: A Critical Survey*. Norman: U of Oklahoma P, 1973. 288–301.

Walsh, Thomas F. "Xochitl: Katherine Anne Porter's Changing Goddess." *American Literature* 52 (1980): 183–93.

Warren, Robert Penn, ed. *Katherine Anne Porter: A Collection of Essays*. Englewood Cliffs, NJ: Prentice Hall, 1979.

—. "Katherine Anne Porter (Irony with a Center)." *Kenyon Review* 4 (1942): 29–42. Rpt. *Katherine Anne Porter*. Edited with an introduction by Harold Bloom. Modern Critical Views. New York: Chelsea House, 1986. 7–21.

—. "Uncorrupted Consciousness: The Stories of Katherine Anne Porter." *Yale Review* 55 (1966): 280–90.

Welty, Eudora. "The Eye of the Story." In *Katherine Anne Porter: A Critical Symposium*, ed. Lodwick Hartley and George Core. Athens: U of Georgia P, 1969. 103–12. Rpt. *Katherine Anne Porter*. Edited with an introduction by Harold Bloom. Modern Critical Views. New York: Chelsea House, 1986. 43–51. Originally appeared in *Yale Review* in 1965.

Wescott, Glenway. "Katherine Anne Porter Personally." In *Katherine Anne Porter: A Critical Symposium*, ed. Lodwick Hartley and George Core. Athens: U of Georgia P, 1969. 24–48.

West, Ray B., Jr. *Katherine Anne Porter*. U of Minnesota Pamphlets on American Writers, no. 28. Minneapolis: U of Minnesota P, 1963.

Wilson, Edmund. "Katherine Anne Porter." *New Yorker* 20 (September 1944): 64–66.

Wolfe, Bertram. *The Fabulous Life of Diego Rivera*. New York: Stein and Day, 1963. 134–38.

Young, Vernon A. "The Art of Katherine Anne Porter." *New Mexico Quarterly* 15 (1945): 326–41.

CRITICISM OF KATHERINE ANNE PORTER'S FICTION

"The Circus" (1935)

Joselyn, Sister M. "Animal Imagery in Katherine Anne Porter's Fiction." In *Myth and Symbol: Critical Ap-*

proaches and Applications, ed. Bernice Slote. Lincoln: U of Nebraska P, 1963. 101–15.

Kaplan, Charles. "True Witness: Katherine Anne Porter." *Colorado Quarterly* 7 (1959): 319–27.

Schwartz, Edward Greenfield. "The Fictions of Memory." *Southwest Review* 45 (1960): 204–15.

"The Cracked Looking-Glass" (1932)

Wiesenfarth, Brother Joseph. "Reflections in 'The Cracked Looking-Glass.'" In *Katherine Anne Porter: A Critical Symposium*, ed. Lodwick Hartley and George Core. Athens: U of Georgia P, 139–48.

"A Day's Work" (1940)

Prescott, Orville. "Books of the Times." *New York Times* (18 Sept. 1944): 17. Maintains that "A Day's Work" is "almost a masterpiece."

"The Downward Path to Wisdom" (1939)

Allen, Charles A. "Katherine Anne Porter: Psychology As Art." *Southwest Review* 41 (1956): 223–30.

Joselyn, Sister M. "Animal Imagery in Katherine Anne Porter's Fiction." In *Myth and Symbol: Critical Approaches and Applications*, ed. Bernice Slote. Lincoln: U of Nebraska P, 1963. 101–15.

"The Fig Tree" (1960)

Hall, Kristen. "'The Fig Tree's' Lessons." *Humanities* 9 (1988): 22–23.

Titus, Mary. "'Mingled Sweetness and Corruption': Katherine Anne Porter's 'The Fig Tree' and 'The Grave.'" *South Atlantic Review* 53 (1988): 111–25.

Schwartz, Edward Greenfield. "The Fictions of Memory." *Southwest Review* 45 (1960): 204–15.

"Flowering Judas" (1930)

Bloom, Harold. Introduction. *Katherine Anne Porter*. Edited with an introduction by Harold Bloom. Modern Critical Views. New York: Chelsea House, 1986. 1–5.

Bluefarb, Sam. "Loss of Innocence in 'Flowering Judas.'" *College Language Association Journal* 7 (1964): 256–62.

Gottfried, Leon. "Death's Other Kingdom: Dantesque and Theological Symbolism in 'Flowering Judas.'" *PMLA* 84 (1969): 112–24.

Gross, Beverly. "The Poetic Narrative: A Reading of 'Flowering Judas.'" *Style* 2 (1968): 129–39.

Liberman, M. M. "Symbolism, the Short Story, and 'Flowering Judas.'" In *Katherine Anne Porter*. Edited with an introduction by Harold Bloom. Modern Critical Views. New York: Chelsea House, 1986. 53–59. Originally a portion of Liberman's *Katherine Anne Porter's Fiction*, 1971.

Redden, Dorothy S. "'Flowering Judas': Two Voices." *Studies in Short Fiction* 6 (1969): 194–204.

Walsh, Thomas F. "The Making of 'Flowering Judas.'" *Journal of Modern Literature* 12 (1985): 109–30.

West, Ray B. "Katherine Anne Porter: Symbol and Theme in 'Flowering Judas.'" In *Katherine Anne Porter: A Critical Symposium*, ed. Lodwick Hartley and

George Core. Athens, GA: U of Georgia P, 1969. 120–28.

"The Grave" (1935)

Brooks, Cleanth. "On 'The Grave.'" *Yale Review* 55 (1966): 175–79.

Cheatham, George. "Literary Criticism, Katherine Anne Porter's 'Consciousness,' and the Silver Dove." *Studies in Short Fiction* 25 (1988): 109–15.

Curley, Daniel. "Treasure in 'The Grave.'" *Modern Fiction Studies* 9 (1963): 377–84.

Gardiner, Judith Kegan. "'The Grave,' 'On Not Shooting Sitting Birds,' and the Female Esthetic." *Studies in Short Fiction* 20 (1983): 265–71.

Joselyn, Sister M., O.S.B. "'The Grave' as Lyrical Short Story." *Studies in Short Fiction* 1 (1964): 216–21.

Rooke, Constance, and Bruce Wallis. "Myth and Epiphany in Porter's 'The Grave.'" In *Katherine Anne Porter*. Edited with an introduction by Harold Bloom. Modern Critical Views. New York: Chelsea House, 1986. 61–68. Originally appeared in *Studies in Short Fiction* in 1978.

Schwartz, Edward Greenfield. "The Fictions of Memory." *Southwest Review* 45 (1960): 204–15.

Titus, Mary. "'Mingled Sweetness and Corruption': Katherine Anne Porter's 'The Fig Tree' and 'The Grave.'" *South Atlantic Review* 53 (1988): 111–25.

"Hacienda" (1932, 1934)

Perry, Robert L. "Porter's 'Hacienda' and the Theme of Change." *Midwest Quarterly* 6 (1965): 403–15.

Simmen, Edward. Introduction. *Gringos in Mexico: One Hundred Years of Mexico in the American Short Story*, ed. Edward Simmen. Fort Worth: Texas Christian UP, 1988. xxxvi–xxxviii.

"He" (1927)

Jorgensen, Bruce W. "'The Other Side of Silence': Katherine Anne Porter's 'He' as Tragedy." In *Katherine Anne Porter*. Edited with an introduction by Harold Bloom. Modern Critical Views. New York: Chelsea House, 1986. 107–15. Originally appeared in *Modern Fiction Studies* in 1982.

Moddelmog, Debra A. "Narrative Irony and Hidden Motivations in Katherine Anne Porter's 'He.'" In *Katherine Anne Porter*. Edited with an introduction by Harold Bloom. Modern Critical Views. New York: Chelsea House, 1986. 117–25. Originally appeared in *Modern Fiction Studies* in 1982.

"Holiday" (1960)

Core, George. "'Holiday': A Version of Pastoral." In *Katherine Anne Porter: A Critical Symposium*, ed. Lodwick Hartley and George Core. Athens: U of Georgia P, 1969. 149–58.

"The Jilting of Granny Weatherall" (1929)

Barnes, Daniel R., and Madeline T. Barnes. "The Secret Sin of Granny Weatherall." *Renascence* 21 (1969): 162–65.

Cobb, Joann. "Pascal's Wager and Two Modern Losers." In *Katherine Anne Porter*. Edited with an introduction by Harold Bloom. Modern Critical Views. New York: Chelsea House, 1986. 97–106. The "two modern losers" are Granny Weatherall in Porter's story, and The Misfit in Flannery O'Connor's "A Good Man Is Hard to Find." Originally appeared in *Philosophy and Literature* in 1979.

Estes, David C. "Granny Weatherall's Dying Moment: Katherine Anne Porter's Allusions to Emily Dickinson." *Studies in Short Fiction* 22 (1985): 437–42.

Wiesenfarth, Brother Joseph. "Internal Opposition in Porter's 'Granny Weatherall.'" *Critique* 11 (1969): 47–55.

Wolfe, Peter. "The Problems of Granny Weatherall." *CLA Journal* 11 (1967): 142–48.

"The Journey" ["The Old Order"] (1936)

Fetterley, Judith. "The Struggle for Authenticity: Growing Up Female in *The Old Order*." *Kate Chopin Newsletter* 2 (1976): 11–19.

Gaston, Edwin W., Jr. "The Mythic South of Katherine Anne Porter." *Southwestern American Literature* 3 (1973): 81–85.

Schwartz, Edward Greenfield. "The Fictions of Memory." *Southwest Review* 45 (1960): 204–15.

"The Last Leaf" (1944)

Schwartz, Edward Greenfield. "The Fictions of Memory." *Southwest Review* 45 (1960): 204–15.

"The Leaning Tower" (1941)

Allen, Charles. "The Nouvelles of Katherine Anne Porter." *University of Kansas City Review* 29 (1962): 87–93.

Young, Vernon A. "The Art of Katherine Anne Porter." *New Mexico Quarterly* 15 (1945): 326–41.

Spencer, Theodore. "Texas and Berlin." *Time* 44 (25 Sept. 1944): 103–04.

Wilson, Edmund. Review of *The Leaning Tower and Other Stories* by Katherine Anne Porter. *New Yorker* 30 Sept. 1944: 64–66.

"Magic" (1928)

Leath, Helen L. "Washing the Dirty Linen in Private: An Analysis of Katherine Anne Porter's 'Magic.'" *CCTE Proceedings* 50 (1985): 51–58.

"María Concepción" (1922)

Hafley, James. "'María Concepción': Life Among the Ruins." *Four Quarters* 12 (1962): 11–17.

"The Martyr" (1923)

Unrue, Darlene H. *Understanding Katherine Anne Porter*. Columbia: U of South Carolina P, 1988. 28–31.

Wolfe, Bertram. *The Fabulous Life of Diego Rivera*. New York: Stein and Day, 1963. 134–38.

"Noon Wine" (1936)

Allen, Charles. "The Nouvelles of Katherine Anne Porter." *University of Kansas City Review* 29 (1962): 87–93.

Leiter, Louis. "The Expense of Spirit in a Waste of Shame: Motif, Montage, and Structure in 'Noon Wine.'" In *Seven Contemporary Short Novels*, ed. Charles Clerc and Louis Leiter. Glenview, IL: Scott Foresman, 1969. 186–219.

Pierce, Marvin. "Point of View: Katherine Anne Porter's 'Noon Wine.'" *Ohio University Review* 3 (1961): 95–113.

Walsh, Thomas F. "Deep Similarities in *Noon Wine*." *Mosaic* 9 (1975): 83–91.

—. "The 'Noon Wine' Devils." *Georgia Review* 22 (1968): 90–96.

"Old Mortality" (1938)

Allen, Charles. "The Nouvelles of Katherine Anne Porter." *University of Kansas City Review* 29 (1962): 87–93.

DeMouy, Jane Krause. "Face to Face: 'Old Mortality.'" In *Katherine Anne Porter*. Edited with an introduction by Harold Bloom. Modern Critical Views. New York: Chelsea House, 1986. 127–39. Originally from DeMouy's *Katherine Anne Porter's Women: The Eye of Her Fiction*, 1983.

Gaston, Edwin W., Jr. "The Mythic South of Katherine Anne Porter." *Southwestern American Literature* 3 (1973): 81–85.

Schwartz, Edward Greenfield. "The Fictions of Memory." *Southwest Review* 45 (1960): 204–15.

Walsh, Thomas F. "Miranda's Ghost in 'Old Mortality.'" *College Literature* 6 (1979–1980): 57–63.

"The Old Order" (1936) (see "The Journey")

The Old Order (1944) [group title for seven collected stories]

Fetterley, Judith. "The Struggle for Authenticity: Growing Up Female in *The Old Order*." *Kate Chopin Newsletter* 2 (1976): 11–19.

Gaston, Edwin W., Jr. "The Mythic South of Katherine Anne Porter." *Southwestern American Literature* 3 (1973): 81–85.

Schwartz, Edward Greenfield. "The Fictions of Memory." *Southwest Review* 45 (1960): 204–15.

"Pale Horse, Pale Rider" (1938)

Allen, Charles. "The Nouvelles of Katherine Anne Porter." *University of Kansas City Review* 29 (1962): 87–93.

Walsh, Thomas F. "The Dream's Self in 'Pale Horse, Pale Rider.'" *Wascana Review* 14 (Fall 1979): 61–79. Rpt. *Katherine Anne Porter*. Edited with an introduction by Harold Bloom. Modern Critical Views. New York: Chelsea House, 1986. 81–95.

Yanella, Philip R. "The Problems of Dislocation in 'Pale Horse, Pale Rider.'" *Studies in Short Fiction* 6 (1969): 637–42.

Youngblood, Sarah. "Structure and Imagery in Katherine Anne Porter's 'Pale Horse, Pale Rider.'" *Modern Fiction Studies* 5 (1959): 344–52.

"Rope" (1928)

Givner, Joan. *Katherine Anne Porter: A Life.* New York: Simon and Schuster, 1982. 174, 221.

Ship of Fools (1962)

Abrahams, William. "Progression through Repetition." *Massachusetts Review* (Summer 1963): 805–08.

Alexander, Jean. "Katherine Anne Porter's Ship in the Jungle." *Twentieth Century Literature* 11 (1966): 180–83.

Corey, Jim. "*Ship of Fools*: Katherine Anne Porter in Decline." *Four Quartets* 34 (1985): 16–24.

Givner, Joan. "The Genesis of *Ship of Fools*." *Southern Literary Journal* 10 (1977): 14–30.

Hartley, Lodwick. "Dark Voyagers: A Study of Katherine Anne Porter's *Ship of Fools*." *University Review* 30 (1963): 83–94.

Heilman, Robert B. "*Ship of Fools*: Notes on Style." *Four Quarters* 12 (1962): 46–55. Rpt. *Katherine Anne Porter*. Edited with an introduction by Harold Bloom. Modern Critical Views. New York: Chelsea House, 1986. 23–34.

Hendrick, George. "Hart Crane Aboard the Ship of Fools: Some Speculations." *Twentieth Century Literature* (April 1963): 3–9.

Hertz, Robert N. "Sebastian Brant and Porter's *Ship of Fools*." *Midwest Quarterly* 6 (1965): 389–401.

Janeway, Elizabeth. "For Katherine Anne Porter, *Ship of Fools* Was a Lively Twenty-Two Year Voyage." *New York Times Book Review* (1 April 1962): 4–5.

Kasten, Maurice. Review of *Ship of Fools*. *Shenandoah* (Summer 1962): 54–61.

Kaufmann, Stanley. Review of *Ship of Fools*. *New Republic* (2 April 1962): 23–25.

Kirkpatrick, Smith. "*Ship of Fools*." *Sewanee Review* 71 (1963): 93–98.

Libermann, M. M. "The Responsibility of the Novelist: The Critical Reception of *Ship of Fools*." *Criticism* 8 (1966): 377–88.

—. "The Short Story as Chapter in *Ship of Fools*." *Criticism* 10 (1968): 65–71.

—. "Some Observations on the Genesis of *Ship of Fools*: A Letter [dated 25 September 1931] from Katherine Anne Porter [to Malcolm Cowley]." *PMLA* 73 (1968): 136–37.

Moss, Howard. "No Safe Harbor." In *Katherine Anne Porter*. Edited with an introduction by Harold Bloom. Modern Critical Views. New York: Chelsea House, 1986. 35–41. Originally appeared in *The New Yorker*.

Schorer, Mark. Review of *Ship of Fools*. *New York Times* 1 April 1962: 1, 5.

Solotaroff, Theodore. "*Ship of Fools* and the Critics." *Commentary* 34 (1962): 277–86.

Thompson, John. "The Figure in the Rose-Red Gown." *Partisan Review* (Fall 1962): 608–12.

"The Source" (1941)

Schwartz, Edward Greenfield. "The Fictions of Memory." *Southwest Review* 45 (1960): 204–15.

Wiesenfarth, Brother Joseph. "Internal Opposition in Porter's 'Granny Weatherall.'" *Critique* 11 (1969): 47–55.

"That Tree" (1934)

Givner, Joan. *Katherine Anne Porter: A Life*. New York: Simon and Schuster, 1982. 234, 239, 287–88.

"Theft" (1929)

Praeger, Leonard. "Getting and Spending: Porter's 'Theft.'" *Perspective* 11 (1960): 230–34.

Stein, William Bysshe. "'Theft': Porter's Politics of Modern Love." *Perspective* 11 (1960): 223–28.

Wiesenfarth, Brother Joseph. "The Structure of Katherine Anne Porter's 'Theft.'" *Cithara* 10 (1971): 64–71.

"Virgin Violeta" (1924)

Givner, Joan. *Katherine Anne Porter: A Life*. New York: Simon and Schuster, 1982. 171–72, 221, 239.

"The Witness" (1944)

Schwartz, Edward Greenfield. "The Fictions of Memory." *Southwest Review* 45 (1960): 204–15.

RELEVANT SCHOLARSHIP ON TEXAS
LITERATURE AND CULTURE

Anderson, John Q., Edwin W. Gaston, and James W. Lee, eds. *Southwestern American Literature: A Bibliography*. Chicago: Swallow Press, 1980.

Bennett, Patrick. *Talking with Texas Writers: Twelve Interviews*. College Station: Texas A&M UP, 1980.

Brown, Steven Ford, ed. *Heart's Invention: On the Poetry of Vassar Miller*. Houston: Ford-Brown & Co., 1988.

Christensen, Paul. "Allowing for Such Talk." In Steven Ford Brown, ed. *Heart's Invention: On the Poetry of Vassar Miller*. Houston: Ford-Brown & Co., 1988. 60–80.

Clifford, Craig. "Horseman, Hang On." In Craig Clifford and Tom Pilkington, eds. *Range Wars: Heated Debates, Sober Reflections, and Other Assessments of Texas Writing*. Dallas: Southern Methodist UP, 1989. 43–57.

Clifford, Craig, and Tom Pilkington, eds. *Range Wars: Heated Debates, Sober Reflections, and Other Assessments of Texas Writing*. Dallas: Southern Methodist UP, 1989.

Colquitt, Betsy. "The Landed Heritage of Texas Writing." In *Texas Country: The Changing Rural Scene*. Ed. Glen E. Lich and Dona B. Reeves-Marquardt. College Station: Texas A&M UP, 1986. 171–89.

Corder, Jim W. *Lost in West Texas*. College Station: Texas A&M UP, 1988.

Dobie, J. Frank. *Guide to Life and Literature of the South-west*. Revised Edition. Dallas: Southern Methodist UP, 1952.

Graham, Don. *Texas: A Literary Portrait*. San Antonio: Corona Publishing, 1985.

Graham, Don, James W. Lee, and William T. Pilkington, eds. *The Texas Literary Tradition: Fiction, Folklore, History*. Austin: University of Texas, 1983. "Selected Bibliography," 209–35.

Greene, A. C. *The Fifty Best Books on Texas*. Dallas: Pressworks Publishing, 1982. An expansion of the *Texas Monthly* article.

—. "The Fifty Best Texas Books." In Craig Clifford and Tom Pilkington, eds., *Range Wars: Heated Debates, Sober Reflections, and Other Assessments of Texas Writing*. Dallas: Southern Methodist UP, 1989. 1–12. Reprinted from the August 1981 issue of *Texas Monthly*.

Heinemann, Alison, ed. *Threads of Texas Literature: A Multi-Cultural Design*. Austin: Texas Circuit, 1980.

Hjerter, Kathleen G., comp. *The Art of Tom Lea*. With an Introduction by William Weber Johnson. College Station: Texas A&M UP, 1989.

Lee, James Ward. *Classics of Texas Fiction*. Afterword by A. C. Greene. Dallas: E-Heart Press, 1987.

—. "The Old South in Texas Literature." In *The Texas Literary Tradition*, ed. Don Graham, James W. Lee, and

William T. Pilkington. Austin: U of Texas, 1983. 46–57.

Lich, Glen E. "Questions about Regional Literature." *Texas College English* 22 (1989): 12–15.

Lich, Glen E., and Dona B. Reeves-Marquardt, eds. *Texas Country: The Changing Rural Scene*. College Station: Texas A&M UP, 1986.

Maclean, Kenneth. "Crying Out: Aloneness and Faith in the Poetry of Vassar Miller." In Steven Ford Brown, ed., *Heart's Invention: On the Poetry of Vassar Miller*. Houston: Ford-Brown & Co., 1988. 81–91.

McComb, David G. *Texas: A Modern History*. Austin: U of Texas P, 1989. The final chapter, "The Texas Mystique," is helpfully suggestive.

McMurtry, Larry. "Ever a Bridegroom: Reflections on the Failure of Texas Literature." In Craig Clifford and Tom Pilkington, eds., *Range Wars: Heated Debates, Sober Reflections, and Other Assessments of Texas Writing*. Dallas: Southern Methodist UP, 1989. 13–41. First published in the 23 October 1981 issue of the *Texas Observer*.

—. *In a Narrow Grave: Essays on Texas*. Albuquerque: U of New Mexico P, 1983. Originally published by Encino Press, Austin, in 1968.

Major, Mabel, and T. M. Pearce. *Southwest Heritage: A Literary History with Bibliographies*. Third Edition. Albuquerque: U of New Mexico P, 1972.

Morris, Celia. "Requiem for a Texas Lady." In Craig Clifford and Tom Pilkington, eds., *Range Wars: Heated Debates, Sober Reflections, and Other Assessments of Texas Writing*. Dallas: Southern Methodist UP, 1989.

O'Connor, Robert F., ed. *Texas Myths*. College Station: Texas A&M UP, 1986.

Owens, William A. "Regionalism and Universality." In *The Texas Literary Tradition: Fiction, Folklore, History*. Ed. Don Graham, James W. Lee, and William T. Pilkington. Austin: U of Texas P, 1983.

Pilkington, Tom. "Herding Words: Texas Literature as Trail Drive." In Craig Clifford and Tom Pilkington, eds., *Range Wars: Heated Debates, Sober Reflections, and Other Assessments of Texas Writing*. Dallas: Southern Methodist UP, 1989. 155–72.

—. *Imagining Texas: The Literature of the Lone Star State*. Boston: American Press, 1981.

Reynolds, Clay. "What Does It Take To Be a Texas Writer?" In Craig Clifford and Tom Pilkington, eds., *Range Wars: Heated Debates, Sober Reflections, and Other Assessments of Texas Writing*. Dallas: Southern Methodist UP, 1989. 69–85.

Simmen, Edward, ed. *Gringos in Mexico: One Hundred Years of of Mexico in the American Short Story*. Preface and Introduction by Edward Simmen. Foreword by John Graves. Fort Worth: Texas Christian UP, 1988.

Smith, Rebecca W. "The Southwest in Fiction." *Saturday Review* 25 (16 May 1942): 13, 37.

Western Literature Association, Sponsor. *A Literary History of the American West*. J. Golden Taylor, Editor-in-Chief. Fort Worth: Texas Christian UP, 1987.

Winegarten, Ruthe. *Texas Women: A Pictorial History, From Indians to Astronauts*. Austin: Eakin Press, 1985.

INDEX